Culturally Speaking:

PROMOTING CROSS-CULTURAL AWARENESS IN A POST-9/11 WORLD

MARY COONS

FOREWORD BY **DR. SAM H. ZAKHEM**

FORMER U.S. AMBASSADOR TO BAHRAIN

Culturally Speaking

By Mary Coons

www.culturallyspeak.com

For information, address inquiries to publisher.

This book may be purchased for educational, business, or sales promotional use.

ISBN 10: 1-59298-239-5
ISBN: 13: 978-159298-239-4

Library of Congress Catalog Number: 2008904371

Book design and layout: Rick Korab, Punch Design, Inc.
Minneapolis, Minnesota, USA • punch-design.com

Editing by Marly Cornell

First Printing 2008

12 11 10 09 08 5 4 3 2 1

Bahrain edition printed in Manama, Kingdom of Bahrain
By Dar Akhbar Al Khaleej Printing & Publishing
www.aak-press.com

U.S. edition printed in the United States of America

Beaver's Pond Press

7104 Ohms Lane, Suite 101
Edina, Minnesota 55439 USA
(952) 829-8818
www.BeaversPondPress.com

To order, visit www.BookHouseFulfillment.com or call 1-800-901-3480. Reseller and special sales discounts available.

CONTENTS

CONTENTS

FOREWORD

In the aftermath of 9/11, as Americans are more concerned about what the American media calls "Islamic radicalism," violence, and terrorism, this book serves to dispel numerous misconceptions that Americans and the Muslim Arabs of Bahrain have about each other. It is a must read that can benefit both of these peoples. Mary Coons cites eleven generalizations that Americans and Bahrainis have about each other, and proves that, in most instances, these generalizations are based on preconceived misconceptions and hype by the media, which most often focuses on the negative and plays upon the fears of the people.

In a world full of tension, discord, and conflict, Mary shows the urgent need for both sides to try to understand and respect each other's culture, religion, tradition, and mores. This is achievable, she states, through education, trade missions, exchange programs, and by opening our borders and our minds to each other. The understanding must go beyond the hype and the generalization circulated about the other in the media. Americans must realize that Bahrainis shun Islamic radicalism and abhor terrorism and are as offended by this violent minority as are Americans. The overwhelming majority of Muslims in the Arab world condemn terrorism as an affront to Islam. Ms. Coons concludes that both sides should attempt to put an end to false generalization, bigotry, and prejudice.

Bahrainis reserve their strongest criticism of America to what they believe is the unqualified and lopsided support for Israel. They are angered by the Israeli harsh treatment of the Palestinians in the occupied territories and in Gaza. Yet, despite their resentment of Israeli excesses, Bahrainis call for dialogue and a negotiated peace in the interests of all concerned. America's unqualified support for Israel, in my view, is the root cause of our problems in the Arab world, in particular, and in the Muslim world in general.

The author chose Bahrain because she is the most familiar with that Kingdom, although Bahrain is not the typical Arab or Muslim country. Bahrain has one of the most tolerant and most democratic governments in the Arab and Muslim world. The ruling family, headed by His Majesty King Hamad bin Isa Al Khalifa, as his late father, His Highness Shaikh Isa bin Salman Al Khalifa before him, has always been pro-American, and has afforded equal rights and protection to their citizens regardless of religion, race, color, or ethnic origin. In testimony, King Hamad appointed Shura Council member Huda Nonoo in May 2008 as the Arab world's first Jewish female ambassador to the United States. The upper chamber of Bahrain's bilateral parliament also has a female Christian member.

It is my hope that this book will be the first of many about the people and governments of Muslim countries. With more than a billion in membership, and the fastest growing religion in the world, Islam is one of the most misunderstood religions in America. We need more dialogue and understanding in order to wipe out hatred and fear. Please pass this book on to a friend.

Dr. Sam H. Zakhem

Former U.S. Ambassador to Bahrain, 1986-89 and
the first Arab-born, Arab-American ambassador
Former Colorado State Representative
Former Colorado State Senator

INTRODUCTION

To many Americans, it seems as though the Islamic world is our enemy. But the Islamic world is not our enemy. *Ignorance* is our enemy.

It is crucial that we listen and understand one another's perspective, and not allow misconceptions to fester. This does not mean we must always agree with these perspectives. But we do have a responsibility to respect one another's opinions as part of healthy, intellectual stimulation.

Culture is like the air we breathe; it cannot be seen, but it is there--and it is essential to life. As individuals of moral character, we have a custodial responsibility to shape and protect our culture. So exactly how do we go about doing that? How do we promote a healthy culture to our children, neighbors, and society as a whole?

Step one is to admit our ignorance, recognize and dispel gross generalizations and, finally, begin to influence and inspire changed attitudes toward cross-cultural differences among family, friends, and coworkers.

Because the Middle East is such a large, diverse region, where the status of women varies significantly from country to country, as does the Islamic culture, this book concentrates on the Arab Muslims of the Kingdom of Bahrain.

When discussing Bahrain, the first question I often hear is, "Where is Bahrain? I've never heard of it."

The Kingdom of Bahrain is an archipelago of thirty-three islands located in the Arabian Gulf (also known as the Persian Gulf) that is connected to Saudi Arabia by a causeway. It has been home to the U.S. Navy's Fifth Fleet for more than fifty years.

Bahrain has a total area of 688 square kilometers (275 square miles), which is three and a half times the size of Washington, DC. As an archipelago, Bahrain does not share a land boundary with another country, but does have a 161-kilometer (100-mile) coastline.

Although the first Gulf state to discover oil (1932), Bahrain's economy has diversified greatly since then. According to the United Nations Economic and Social Commission for Western Asia, Bahrain has the fastest growing economy in the Arab world. The 2005 United Nations World Investment report proclaimed the Kingdom as the first country to attract direct foreign investment in the Gulf, thus ranking twenty-seventh globally. Bahrain is now widely recognized as *the* financial hub of the Middle East.

In addition, the Kingdom has the freest economy of seventeen countries in the Middle East. In 2007, Bahrain was ranked the nineteenth freest country in the world, according to the 2008 Index of Economic Freedom, published by the Heritage Foundation/*Wall Street Journal* (www.heritage.org/index). According to these results, Bahrain became one of the Arabian Gulf's most advanced economies and most progressive political systems after gaining its independence from Great Britain in 1971.

Of the population, now greater than one million, 529,446 are Bahrainis and 517,368 represent the global expatriate community throughout the world. The ten-year population census, released in January 2008, indicates a 5.7 percent increase.

An Islamic country where 85 percent of the Bahraini society practices Islam, 60-65 percent of Bahrainis are Shia. The ruling family is Sunni. Other welcomed and practicing faiths include Christianity, Hinduism, Judaism, and Buddhism. Bahrain is known for its authentic Arab heritage and reputation for being relatively liberal and modern.

Bahrain has been ruled by the Al Khalifa family since 1783. The country is a constitutional monarchy that gained full independence from the UK in 1971.

His Majesty King Hamad bin Isa Al Khalifa ascended to the throne in March 1999 following the death of his father. The government is led by His Highness Shaikh Khalifa bin Salman Al Khalifa, the prime minister, and His Highness Shaikh Salman bin Hamad Al Khalifa, the Crown Prince and the King's eldest son. (Al correlates to family, bin means son of; therefore, His Highness Shaikh Salman is the son of Hamad of the Khalifa family.)

My firsthand experience within Bahrain began in December 2005 when I visited my husband who was working in the Kingdom. I had no idea where exactly in the Middle East this Muslim country was located. My "experience" was quickly transformed into "emersion." I came to Bahrain with no preconceived expectations. I viewed that initial two-week trip as simply an adventure and an experience that I probably would never have a chance to repeat. Since then, however, I have made eleven trips to the Kingdom staying four to five weeks at a time. By no means an expert on its culture, I have nevertheless listened, observed, asked questions, read voraciously, and met and made new friends.

Some aspects of this culture's social fabric remain confusing, such as its ongoing debate over whether Muslim women should or should not be veiled and cloaked (and in heat-absorbing black yet!), while others are merely unfamiliar religious customs, such as Ramadan, that are better understood while living in Bahrain. I am reminded nevertheless that many Muslim Arabs in Bahrain share a similar confusion about Americans and some of our social practices and behaviors.

With more than one billion Muslims, Islam is the fastest growing religion in the world and, undoubtedly, the most misunderstood. The average American is unfamiliar with how the Arab Muslim culture is integrated within its religion. The Bahraini Arabs mistakenly assume American views are controlled by special interest groups that are opposed to Islam.

In our post-9/11 world, damaging stereotypes and false generalizations swirl. Despite the fact that public polls indicate Americans' new willingness and interest in learning about Arab Muslims and their fabric of society, many myths and misconceptions thrive.

There is profound ignorance on both sides between what we know to be true and what we choose to believe. I will address the most prevalent generalizations, which arose through interviews with both Americans and Bahraini Arabs, and try to dispel the most rabid inaccuracies.

History has shown that a lack of knowledge breeds ignorance; ignorance breeds mistrust; mistrust breeds fear; fear breeds strife, and strife breeds hatred. Life is just too short and precious to be held captive by hatred.

Since humanity continues to be persecuted in the name of religion, region, nationality, and language, it is a commendable contribution to strive toward harmony. Despite the significant differences in religion, politics, and culture, America and Bahrain share the most common desires for humanity; peace, respect, love of family, aspiration, and sustenance. How wonderful it would be if we all extended an olive branch of harmony and respect, regardless of cultural and religious beliefs, when meeting and discussing one another's society.

Mary Coons

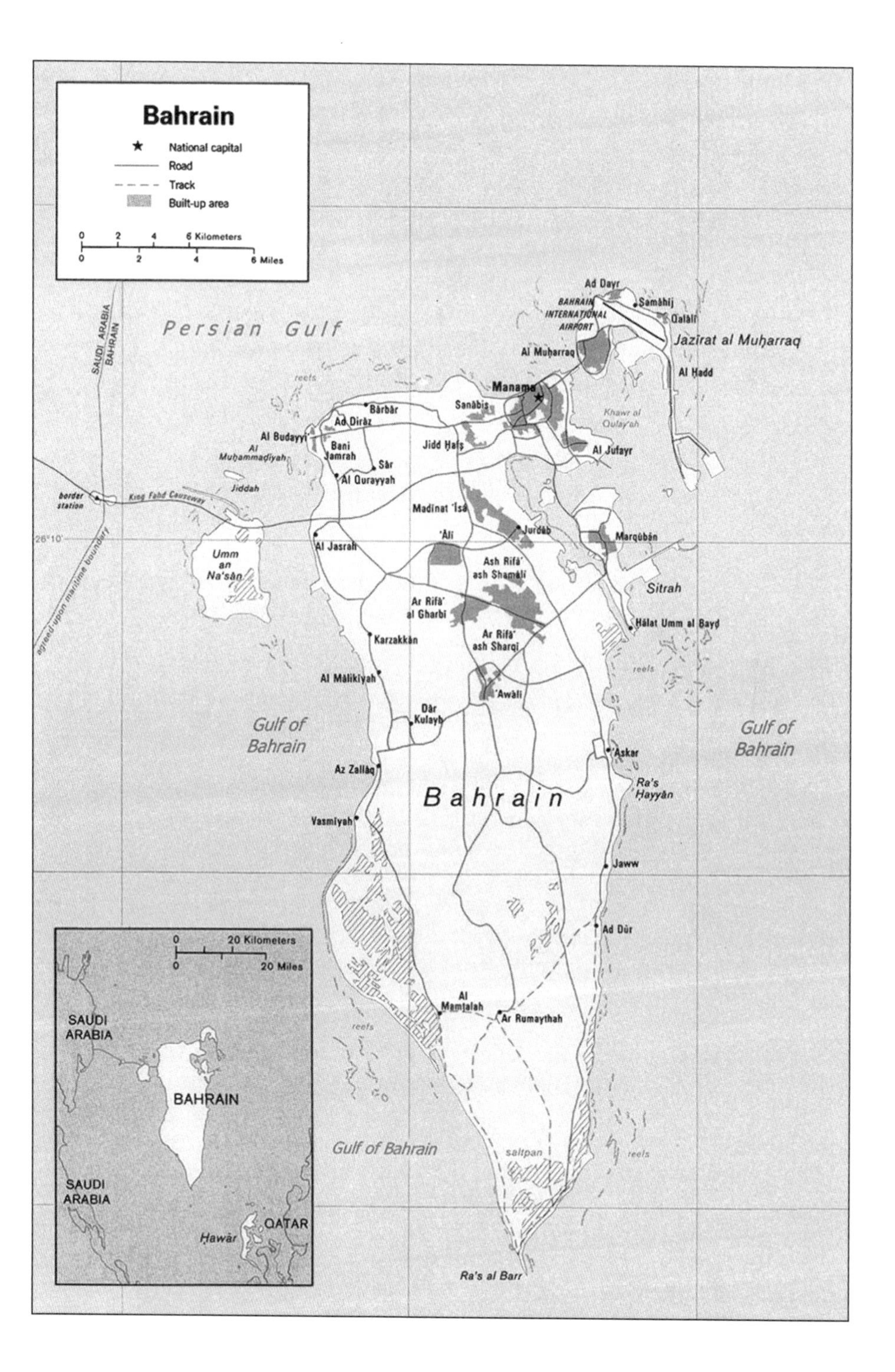
Bahrain
National capital
Road
Track
Built-up area
0 2 4 6 Kilometers
0 2 4 6 Miles
Persian Gulf
SAUDI ARABIA
BAHRAIN
Ad Dayr
Samāhīj
BAHRAIN INTERNATIONAL AIRPORT
Qalālī
Jazīrat al Muḩarraq
Al Muḩarraq
Al Ḩadd
Manama
Sanābis
Bārbār
Ad Dirāz
Khawr al Qulay'ah
Al Budayyi'
Bani Jamrah
Jidd Ḩafş
Al Jufayr
Al Muḩammadīyah
Sār
Al Qurayyah
Jiddah
border station
King Fahd Causeway
Madīnat 'Īsá
Jurdāb
'Ālī
Marqūbān
Al Jasrah
Umm an Na'sān
Ash Rifā' ash Shamālī
Sitrah
agreed-upon maritime boundary
Ar Rifā' al Gharbī
Hālat Umm al Bayḑ
Karzakkān
Ar Rifā' ash Sharqī
reefs
Al Mālikīyah
'Awālī
Dār Kulayb
Gulf of Bahrain
Gulf of Bahrain
'Askar
Az Zallāq
Ra's Ḩayyān
Bahrain
Vasmīyah
Jaww
Ad Dūr
Al Mamtalah
Ar Rumaythah
reefs
Gulf of Bahrain
saltpan
reefs
Ra's al Barr
0 20 Kilometers
0 20 Miles
SAUDI ARABIA
BAHRAIN
SAUDI ARABIA
QATAR
Ḩawār

BAHRAINI ARAB MUSLIMS' GENERALIZATIONS ABOUT AMERICANS

1

America has no respect for its women, as evidenced by advertisements, movies, TV, and pornography.

2

The American culture has destroyed the family system/family values, and they (Americans) have no morals.

3

Western culture is very lax regarding women's clothing that gives mixed messages to men.

4

Americans believe that Muslim women who cover themselves are backward.

5

American students are expected to take a part-time job in high school and move out when they graduate or turn eighteen.

6

Americans are overly concerned with money and profitability.

7

Americans are very good at giving money for humanitarian efforts, but they are also very good at killing people. It's as though they are trying to find a balance for their guilt.

8

The American government has created problems in the world just to have power and political clout worldwide. America can't be trusted.

9

Every decision made by the American government is made with Israel's benefit in mind. The American government is highly influenced by Israel.

10

The American media shows and tells Americans only what the media wants them to know.

11

Americans know nothing about Bahrain, or even where Bahrain is. They probably think we still live in tents in the desert and ride camels.

AMERICANS' GENERALIZATIONS ABOUT THE BAHRAINI ARAB MUSLIMS

1

Islam is a radical, backward religion.

2

Islam is a violent religion that promotes violence and preaches death.

3

Women who veil themselves are forced to and are oppressed. And those who completely veil themselves look scary.

4

Arabs hate Americans, but they sure want an American education.

5

Muslim women are not treated equally with Muslim men, and do not have the same rights, particularly in the workplace and court system.

6

Americans prefer to focus on the future, whereas Muslims seem to live in the past.

7

All Arabs living in oil-producing countries are rich.

8

Arab Muslims hate Israelis.

9

Before 9/11, the Middle East seemed to be in another time. We never saw anything but camels and desert. After 9/11, nineteen terrorists became the face of the entire Arab world.

10

Arabs as a whole are judged as terrorists and radicals, because this is what is in the news.

11

Muslims think Americans are not tolerant of their religion or their culture, particularly post 9/11.

DEDICATION

Although many people provided me with assistance and encouragement, it was Sheikh Mobarak Alsuwaiket of Al Khobar, Kingdom of Saudi Arabia who first planted this book's seed.

I remember his chilling words one sweltering hot day in Saudi—that such a book, promoting cross-cultural awareness and tolerance, was too late for Iraq, but it wasn't too late for Saudi Arabia. Although this book does not address Saudi culture and religion, I hope it is never too late for Saudi Arabia or any other Arabian Gulf country.

My thanks to Sheikh Mobarak.

ACKNOWLEDGMENTS

Without the willingness and cooperation of those Americans and Bahrainis who allowed me to interview them and shared so much about their personal lives, this book would not have been possible.

I also thank Maryam al Sherooqi of Wide Horizon Event Planning & Management, Kingdom of Bahrain (www.wdhorizon.com)
for her hard work and dedicated assistance in helping me find sponsorship for my book within the Kingdom.

›It is not important if
I am Sunni or Shia;
I am Muslim.
It is not important if
you are Catholic or Protestant;
you are Christian.
We all believe in the same God.‹

Abdul Rasool Mansoor Hassan

CHAPTER 1

The Religion of Islam

Islam and Christianity are not as globally different as one might first think. In fact, there are many similarities.

Muslims believe in the one true God as the creator, in the angels He created, in the prophets through whom His revelations were brought to mankind, in the Day of Judgment and individual accountability for one's actions, in God's complete authority over human destiny, and in life after death. (Muslims often interchange the word Allah, which is Arabic for Almighty God, with the word God.)

Muslims believe in many of the same prophets as Christians starting with Adam and including, but not limited to: Noah, Abraham, Isaac, Jacob, Moses, David, Solomon, John the Baptist, and Jesus. They believe that these prophets were sent by God to convey a universal message: The true God is only one. Worship Him alone and keep His commandments. Similar to Catholicism, Muslims hold Mary (Maryam in Arabic), the mother of Jesus, in high esteem.

A major difference in the two religions is the Islamic belief that God's message to man was revealed to Prophet Muhammad, when he was about forty years old, in the form of the Quran through the Angel Gabriel, and that Muhammad is the last messenger of God to mankind. Christians believe the Bible is the word of God and that Jesus is the messenger of God, as well as the Son of God. Islam does not believe that God is the Father, the Son, and the Holy Spirit as Christian dogmas profess. The Prophet Muhammad always emphasized that he was only a mortal man with the mission of preaching and obeying God's message, and not an intermediary of God. By the time he died in A.D. 632, Prophet Muhammad had unified all Arabia, and Islam had already begun its sweep of the Near East. Abu Bakr,

Muhammad's father-in-law, was chosen as his interim successor (caliph) in the political and religious arena, and he was accepted by nearly all of Muhammad's followers.

According to Islamic scholars, Islam, which means a state of being, implies peace, safety, submission, acceptance, and surrender. Through this submission, the peace, security, and wholesome well-being implied in its literal meaning are achieved. A Muslim's Islam weakens through sin, ignorance, and wrongdoing, or if he does not worship God alone. Muhammad stressed that one of his message's chief goals was to provide a guide to proper manners and upright behavior.

Islam, which originated in Saudi Arabia some fourteen hundred years ago, preaches that the Quran's message of divine scripture is God's exact words conveyed to Prophet Muhammad in Arabic through the archangel Gabriel. Muhammad was instructed to reveal the Quran's scripture, through himself and his followers, to all humanity for their guidance and salvation. Furthermore, Islam believes that the Quran's message was revealed in a series of revelations to the Prophet Muhammad over a period of twenty-three years. Because the revelations were written down during his lifetime, and because Muslims memorized the teachings in the Quran word for word, they believe the Quran was perfectly preserved.

Islam was born into the Arab culture, which simply means that there was a culture before the religion. The religion adopted some aspects of the Saudi Arabian Arab culture, while other aspects were imposed.

The Arabic word "Muslim" literally means "someone who is in a state of Islam" (submission to the will and law of God). It is a common misconception that Islam is a religion for only Arabs. The Arab world starts at Iraq and the Arabian Gulf. Iranians are not Arabs; their language is different, they are a much older race and, historically, are recent converts to Islam. Although most Arabs are Muslims, there are also Arabs who are Christians, Jews, and atheists. In fact, more than eighty percent of the world's Muslims are not Arabs. The largest Muslim nation in the world is Indonesia where the interpretation of Islam is very different from Bahrain's. Religion is practiced in different ways worldwide, whether Christianity or Islam.

With more than one billion Muslims today, Islam is the fastest growing religion in the world. In France, Belgium, and Spain, Islam is the second largest religious group after Roman Catholics. In Norway and Sweden, Islam is again the second largest religious group after Lutherans. In Bulgaria and Russia, after Orthodox Christians, Islam is the second largest religious group.

Non-Muslims often hear the term the "five pillars of faith" that Muslims ascribe to, but may not understand exactly what those pillars reflect. As part of the Islam religion, all true Muslims must perform five duties, which comprise the Five Pillars of Faith.

Shahada (affirmation)
The duty to recite the creed: "There is nothing worthy of worship save Allah, and Muhammad is the Messenger of God."

Salat (prayer)
The duty to worship the One God in prayer five times each day.

Zakat (almsgiving)
The duty to give away alms and to help the needy.

Siyam (fasting)
The duty to keep the Fast of Ramadan.

Hajj (pilgrimage)
The duty to make the pilgrimage to Mecca at least once in a lifetime.

Islam's holy day is observed on Friday with mosque, while American Christians typically attend church services on Sunday.

Muslims are forbidden to eat pork, as most Americans know. According to the Quran, God says that pigs are a dirty diseased animal, but a specific reason that pork is forbidden is not given. Many Muslims I spoke with agreed that there was a reason for this ruling and, although it may be unclear to them, obedience to this ruling is a matter of faith. God said do not eat pork, so they do not.

Rasool Hassan, a Bahraini-born Muslim who has lived in the Kingdom of Bahrain his entire life, explained what being Muslim means to him: "I'm not Sunni or Shia; I am Muslim. That is what I tell people when they ask me which I am. Someone asked my Christian friend once if he was Catholic. He answered that he was Christian, not Catholic or Protestant. It is not important if I am Sunni or Shia; I am Muslim. It is not important if you are Catholic or Protestant; you are Christian. We all believe in the same God."

"We have good relations with Christians," added Hameed Alawi, a Shia Muslim. "Islam allows us to marry Christian girls. There are so many similarities between the two religions. I know that Americans are kind and respectful of other religions. I saw that during the three years that I lived and worked with Americans."

Vatican officials announced that Catholic and Muslim representatives planned to meet in Rome in the spring of 2008 to begin an "historic" dialogue between the faiths and to develop their common ground—belief in one God.

How the Sunni and Shia Sects Differ

There are two kinds of Arab Muslims – Sunni and Shia – who have lived amongst each other for centuries. In Bahrain, they tolerate each other for the most part and, although each has its own, they are free to attend the other's mosques. There is no segregation between the two sects in terms of geography and where they might choose to live or shop. There are pockets of neighborhoods in Bahrain where a majority may live; a practice that the United States is very familiar with, dating back to early immigration times when certain ethnic groups located to a particular part of a city.

The theological difference between these two main Islamic branches stems from who is the "rightful" successor of the Prophet Muhammad. The Shia (or Shiites) believe the caliph (the Muslim spiritual leader) descends through Muhammad and his descendents, and son-in-law Ali, who they believe Muhammad personally chose, to be his successor. The Shia believe the early caliphs should not only rule, but also interpret the Quran.

The Sunnis reject this concentration of religious power. They believe that Muhammad's role in revealing God's laws in the Quran ended with him, and that caliphs held mainly political power.

Both groups believe in the five pillars of Islam. Although some rituals and forms of prayer have developed differently over the centuries, the prayers are the same. Both celebrate the same holidays: marking the end of Ramadan, the end of the hajj, Muhammad's birth date, and the death of Ali's son, Hussein.

According to Hameed Alawi, "The donging [call], also known as adhan, is ten or fifteen minutes different between the two. Shia used to pray using a stone, which was a habit from Prophet Muhammad who used part of the earth to pray on. The Sunni do not use this stone. Their prayer styles are slightly different; Sunnis fold their arms while praying and Shia hold them down at their sides." Alawi said that the Bahraini government assigned two management branches to address misunderstandings and issues between the two groups. The management of the government assigned to help the Shia is called Jaffari Court, and Sunni Court for the Sunnis.

Although mixed marriage among Sunni and Shia families is permitted, Alawi admits that it has become more difficult in the last five years or so in Bahrain due to issues that have become more prominent. Sunni families I spoke with agreed. The predominant issue cited was concern about whether the children from a marriage between a Shiite and a Sunni will be Sunni or Shia. Most families here avoid this quandary. Furthermore, the Shia disapprove of divorce, and it is very difficult for them to obtain one; whereas, it is easier for Sunnis to divorce.

Salah al Shuroogi, a Sunni male, provided some historic background information, explaining that the Shia came two to three hundred years after Islam, which is why the majority of (more than one billion) Muslims worldwide are Sunni compared to less than one hundred thirty million Shia.

"The Shia are mainly concentrated in Iran," he said, "But they are not ministers, managers, or officers of the Army. In Bahrain the Sunnis were always the majority because of British colonization. Because the British wanted the Shia as "allies," they brought some twenty thousand Shia families from Iran and Iraq to Bahrain. One group came in the 1930s or '40s, and another group in the beginning of the 1970s. That's how the Shia arrived in Bahrain."

"There is also a difference between the two groups of Shia," he continued. "The original Shia are those who have been living with us for thousands of years, and the new Shia came in the twentieth century. These new Shia are now asking for the United Nations to re-vote for Bahrain to become an Iranian colony. That's the difference between the old and new Shia."

Americans are curious about whether one can differentiate between a Sunni and a Shia, so I put the question to Hameed. He explained, "You, of course, could never tell. I will recognize maybe eighty percent of them. In Bahrain the Shia and Sunni have different Arabic accents. Because I live here, I also am aware of their difference in dress, although sometimes I cannot know. About ninety percent of Shia women will have their hair covered, whereas I'd say maybe sixty or seventy percent of Sunni girls cover their's. Both wear the abaya, but I think Shia wear it more often than Sunni girls. The Sunni skin color is generally a bit darker also."

I have had Arabs proudly tell me that they are "pure Bahraini." Not sure what this meant, I asked a Sunni Arab. He explained that if one can trace his ancestors back to the Arab Bedouins of Bahrain, then he is "pure Bahraini."

AMERICAN Generalization #1

Islam is a radical and backward religion.

"It is our belief that Islam is a completion of Christianity, because we believe in Moses and the other prophets that Christians believe in. If we are radicals, then that means other religions are radical also. I don't think Islam is radical, although you find radicals everywhere – even in the States. So, no, I don't feel this generalization is a deserving statement," Rasool Hassan told me.

"I don't blame Americans for thinking this," said Wafaa Ashoor, a Sunni Muslim woman. "This is what they saw. So now they need to see the other side."

I was fortunate to meet an American woman, Lee Ann Fleetwood, a former Christian married to a Bahraini Arab Muslim, who converted to Islam. As an American who initially knew nothing of Islam and had been living in Bahrain for twenty years, she agreed to share her experiences in the hope that Americans might more easily understand the Islamic religion and its beliefs.

"A lot of people assume that if you are a Christian married to a Muslim, you will convert to Islam, which many do just to make their lives easier," Fleetwood said. "I was married about two years before I converted. Although my husband's family was Muslim, they were not strictly practicing Islam. I was surprised that, for being an Islamic country, there was no information out there twenty years ago. Those interested in Islam might go to Discover Islam for booklets, but there was really nothing in depth about the Islamic religion in Bahrain. So when I first came here, I had no incentive to learn about Islam. Of course, back then it was also difficult to find books in English; most bookstores only carried books in Arabic. I came across an English version of the Quran and, sort of against my will, I read it. Surprisingly, I agreed with every thing I read, and it was easy to follow and practice.

"But let's say that in America someone becomes interested in Islam for whatever reason," she continued. "Usually the first thing they will read is the Quran to learn about the religion. This is where the true, accurate information is found. So most Americans would decide whether to convert or not based on what they read in the Quran. But I learned Islam by the behavior and actions of other Muslims, which was culture-based Islam versus Quran-based Islam. The two are very intermingled. When you grow up in Islam, you learn your culture right along with Islam. I have had many disagreements with Bahraini-born Muslims over this because I was a Westerner who came to Bahrain as an adult outsider – and still Christian – although married to a Bahraini Arab Muslim. I had the advantage of seeing both sides of this culture and religion.

"When you become a Muslim, you don't become an individual Muslim following God," emphasized Fleetwood. "You become a Muslim of Islam, a worldwide society. You are accepted as a brother and sister to all the other

Muslims on the planet in this society-based religion. Yes, you should be concerned about your family, and your neighbor, and the sick and poor as to their well being, but where I have an issue with Islam is when the Arab culture becomes overbearing and tries pushing its beliefs onto everyone around it. I am an individual even though I am Muslim, and I should be able to practice or not practice, or believe or not believe, what fits and satisfies me. But you can't do that when you live within this Arab culture. I am expected to follow what the Arab Muslims here want me to follow, and my children are to follow it as well. That is what I do not accept. They want me immersed into their culture as well as their religion."

Fleetwood illustrated her point further by explaining her opinion about the difference between the Quran and the Hadith. "According to Muslims, the Quran is the word of God. Everything in here is the direct word from God to us. We view it as a manual that teaches us what to do and what to avoid. Anything that is not in there might come from another source called the Hadith. Muslims often go to the Hadith to learn additional things. Much of the Islamic-practiced Arab culture comes from the Hadith."

It is important to distinguish between religion and culture as they are intertwined, yet also two very separate things. Fleetwood maintained that, "If it's in the Quran, it is religion, and if it's in the Hadith, it is a mix of religion and culture. Much of what is in the Hadith is the prophet's personal beliefs and habits. As an Arab, he had Arab habits. A lot of the Hadith is based on the prophet's personal life, which is culture-based. To be very simplistic, Arab is a culture, and Muslim is a religion."

Native Bahraini Maryam al Sheroogi offered an opposing view. "For me, culture and religion are one. My culture came from my religion, and Hadith has come to support the Quran by expanding on it. After the Quran, the Hadith is next in importance. So I believe we cannot separate the Hadith from the Quran. This is the culture and you can't change it, nor do I want to change it."

American democracy prescribes to "government of the people, by the people, and for the people," as stated in the U.S. Constitution. In Islam it is God, and not the people, who dictates a government's legitimacy, with Muslim countries conforming to Islamic laws. This is a very strange concept to Americans who are accustomed to a distinct separation of church and state.

Many Americans, and those from European countries as well, expect that as Muslim societies develop economically, they will somehow separate religion from politics – or at least from the public realm – and treat Islam more as a private thing. However, that has not happened. In fact, as Muslim societies modernize and evolve, those societies and countries appear to have an even greater attachment to Islam. For Muslims, (I have been told), religion can never be a purely private matter. Political Islam is alive and well in the Kingdom of Bahrain.

The Bedouin Arabs Prior to Islam

The Arab woman in Arabia, before Islam, was very much subjugated, according to Dr. Mansoor Al Jamri, editor-in-chief of Bahrain's leading Arab daily newspaper, *Alwasat News*. "That was the very male-dominated culture before Islam – the Bedouin culture. There is another fact of which Arabs do not talk about. Before Islam, eight months of the year were considered free of laws; therefore, thefts, rape, and plundering were common practice. During those other four months, you were not allowed to steal, raid another tribe, and so on. Therefore, it was very logical that the more you covered and protected your women, the safer they were. Islam promulgated cutting the hands of thieves at that time and, although few hands were severed, those uncivilized habits came to an end.

"A woman could not travel alone on a camel between villages," he continued, "Because there may be thieves around who might attack and rape her. Therefore, she needed protection unless she was a warrior. And there were some women warriors, but usually they were men. So these traditions came before Islam, and Islam responded to them adequately.

"Prior to Islam, women did not inherit. A woman was to be owned. When Islam was founded, it gave women half of the inheritance. So from that perspective," suggested Al Jamri, "It was a step up. If you look at the time and place when women were not recognized as owners of property, Islam gave her ownership. So it was the first time in Arabia that women began to own things. Islam gave her this respect."

According to Al Jamri, some traditions have remained because of the Bedouin culture. "The Arabs wore two caps; the Bedouin and Hadhar (settled). The Bedouins were moving all the time. Then they were living in hadhar – a town-like environment – where civility would predominate. One problem that resulted was this mixture of tribishin, which had come back after Islam and remained in the deserts. When the oil came, material lives were upgraded, but the cultural life stayed as it had been."

Salifism

"In the 1980s another Muslim trend developed, which was the salifist [school of thought] similar to what the Puritans were in American history," explained Al Jamri. "The salifists are the Puritans of the Muslims who came to Bahrain mainly from Saudi Arabia. The salifists believe they must revert back to pure Islam teachings to solve our problems. Some of them advocated peaceful means, but others advocated force. This was their theological background. Osama bin Laden came from the Bedouin salifist group that advocated force.

"In 1979, some of the salifists overtook Mecca, the holiest place in Islam. The Saudis forcibly killed them in Mecca. After that, the Saudis wanted rid of the salifist presence in Saudi politics, so they provided the salifists with money, facilities, and schools and asked them to go outside of Saudi Arabia and teach. Then, in 1980 when the Soviets invaded Afghanistan, the Saudis allowed these salifists to go and make jihad in Afghanistan.

"So this salifist school was created by exporting many religious educators from Saudi Arabia. Weapons and military intelligence came from America. The intent was there, especially for Saudis who told the salifists, 'if you want jihad, go to Afghanistan and kill the infidels. The Communists don't believe in God, so go teach there.'

"Because the Americans wanted to defeat the Soviet Union, they provided the intelligence, weapons, and infrastructure to help the salifist groups in Afghanistan. And therefore, what they did was convert most of the young and place them in religious school training camps on the Pakistan and

Afghanistan border. But these border camps had CIA and American military people training them, with Saudi money and the religious education from Saudi, with the intention of attacking the Soviet Union. They became so powerful, they entered Afghanistan and toppled the Soviet-backed regime, and the Soviets pulled out. So with American help, they achieved their victory.

"Those who controlled Afghanistan were called Taliban, which means 'religious students.' These were students from the religious schools financed by Saudi Arabia and from the training camps run by the Pakistani and American trainers. Therefore, in the 1980s, there existed one united front: the American intelligence, the American military, Saudi money, and the salifists that created Taliban.

"Then Saddam Hussein took over Kuwait in 1990, and the Americans brought a half million Marines and soldiers into Saudi Arabia to liberate Kuwait. This was a turning point for the salifist movement. Bin Laden and his groups appeared on the scene after the Americans came to liberate Kuwait.

"First of all, when the salifists came, the Americans and everyone else had abandoned the Taliban in Afghanistan. So after defeating the Soviets, the salifists also abandoned the Taliban who were fighting and killing each other.

"Secondly, the Americans are now in Saudi Arabia. According to the Puritan salifists, this is a pure land. To bring soldiers into Saudi to control the situation in Arabia is like allowing non-Muslims into the holy Saudi cities of Medinah and Mecca. They promptly switched from fighting Soviets to fighting Americans. They said America had stained the pure land of Arabia, and because the Saudis had invited infidels into Arabia – remember these are puritans and puritanical thinking – the enemy now became the United States of America.

"By now the salifists were very sophisticated in terms of financial networks," continued Al Jamri. "Do you know how many religious schools in Pakistan they run? Twenty-six thousand schools today [2008], and all are outside of state control. Do you know how many students today live in this school? One million!

"These elementary religious schools are teaching children that issues are either black or white. This is halal [permitted] and this is haram [forbidden]. Once financed by Saudi Arabia, now they are self-sustaining. They have training camps everywhere. And remember, Americans trained some of their leaders in the 1980s to fight the Soviets. The Salifists are very sophisticated.

"And out of this came Al Qaeda. Al Qaeda means 'the base'—a base where people are trained and then exported to fight the enemy. Al Qaeda was created out of the forces in Afghanistan that were once a single united force.

"Now, as I said, the enemy is the United States of America. Al Qaeda could bring British Muslims, train them in one of these Pakistani religious schools, and the Pakistani government could do nothing about it. Every religious school has a mosque, and basically every religious school belongs to a mosque with an imam [teacher]. What the Americans and Saudis helped to do was convert Pakistanis, who are very moderate Muslims, into salifists. What happened was the political and religious intermixed, and something slipped.

"We are left with arguments; nobody justifies terrorism. But terrorism is the result of a mismatch between modernity, development, and lack of freedom. The political factor played a part in that. American interests played a part; then they were abandoned. These people then planned and slipped into other countries planning to come back and hunt the Americans down.

"So I believe that America contributed to what happened. We Arabs in the Gulf are living in a most unenlightened environment. But much of it is a mixture of doings. The Americans thought this was the way, and we Arabs have suffered.

"Our wealth in our countries has suffered. Thirty-five percent of the Gulf's governments' budgets go to military and defense, not to health and education. It may be thirty percent in Bahrain now. And we are not spending money educating our people. We could have instructors from Harvard University; Bahrain could even build a Harvard University from the money they spend on military and defense. So the priorities have been defense and security, but defense and security of what?

"Now you find people who are super rich and super sophisticated, but they do not believe in modernity. They use money in their hands to destroy the enemy, whether the enemy is Soviets or Americans."

Political Islam

Sunni businessman Abdulla al Sada asserted that Islam is becoming more and more powered by politics. "Some leaders use Islam as their cloth just to show things in a different way, and for their own benefit. I think that is what is happening now in Bahrain and the other Gulf countries and has been for the past twenty years or so. Some people are changing their beliefs. Muslims are becoming stricter. They are adding something to Islam that is not Islam, for their own political agenda. As a result, we have no clear direction. I see the new generation floundering and lost with no clear direction.

"We are an Arabic country. Then why don't we speak Arabic exclusively instead of Arabic and English? Persians use their language; the French speak French. We are using a different language [English], while we have our own. I'm not saying I want to return to that, but I want a clear focus. We say something and then do something different. The Americans and British have always had clear direction."

Al Sada pointed out that within the last two decades, for example, conflicts between Muslims themselves existed. "This is not Islam; this is something new," he contended. "Islam is salaam, and salaam means peace. What's happening in Iraq is not peace. Men, women, and children are being brainwashed to become suicide bombers. Why did something like 9/11 never happen twenty years ago? Why has it never happened in an Islamic country? If you look at history, you see the Islamic territories stretch from China to the French territory and to all of Africa. These Muslims have never killed. This is Islam. Why are there churches, temples, and mosques everywhere in the Middle East? Why don't Muslims destroy them? Muslims have lived in peace for thousands of years; it is only recently that they have begun killing themselves – the Sunnis and Shia in Iraq, for example. Before there was no reason to kill each other; now there is a reason.

"Globalization is that reason. Multinational companies want to control the market. And they are now controlling worldwide political markets."

Furthermore, according to al Sada, people today are viewing globalization as some new thing. "Globalization existed for thousands of years; this is nothing new. The new thing is the politics behind globalization – the high powers in the world who want to control everything – the economy, the culture, the language – which has made globalization very competitive." In some ways it is good, he admitted, while in other ways it is negative. Al Sada expressed concern that Bahrain's new generation doesn't feel they have their own world or culture. "We are taking a little from here and a little from there," he explained. "It's neither good or bad; rather, society and culture are so open that maybe in the future Arabs will lose their identity; especially those in the Gulf."

Who Interprets the Quran?

Are radical clerics interpreting the Quran the way they want to advance their own agenda? With suicide bombings a near-daily occurrence in war-torn Iraq, what are these clerics saying about this violence? Islam is supposed to be a peaceful religion.

"The Quran is interpreted by a religious elite who have, in my opinion, political agendas," said Nader Shaheen, an Arab Muslim born in England to a Bahraini Arab father and an English mother. "Islam is the only one of the world's religions that offers a political medium. It does not separate church from state. Let's not forget that the Reformation in Europe took four hundred years and cost millions of lives, but that was a move to separate the politics of how people are ruled from the administration of their spiritual needs, whereas Rome wanted very much to keep that all together. If you controlled the people's spiritual leaders, then you owned their politics, too. That's one of the reasons why Britain (and Martin Luther in Germany) opposed the Papacy. But all of this had to happen because there was the seat of Christian power, that did not recognize borders, that could raise an army of four hundred fifty thousand to go "liberate" the Holy Land. That had nothing to do with nationality, or countries, or politics per se, because they were one and the same. It just meant the Papacy became the most potent political power.

"So here we are in 1428, with the death of the prophet, and an elite bunch of clerics who can throw all kinds of religion at you if you politically oppose them. The combination of politics and religion is ideal as a way of managing people and controlling the masses. These are the men who interpret the Quran. These too are men with political agendas (Branch Davidians, Quakers, Seventh Day Adventists, The Church of Latter Day Saints, Catholics, Calvinists, Lutherans, Greek and Russian Orthodox), and they are not Muslim."

Shaheen's point is that someone with a charismatic personality and agenda can interpret God's word to benefit his own ends. "It's this interpretation that people need to be very clear on," he stressed. "You get some people who will find an Islamic cleric who says yes, suicide bombing; absolutely. But Muslims by and large hold the same view of suicide as do Catholics. If you commit suicide, you cannot be buried on hollow ground. Suicide is the surest ticket to hell, and Islam does not condone suicide."

"There is a misconception that Islam was built on the sword and all we want to do is fight," said Fatima Ali, a young Bahraini college graduate whose post-secondary education took her to Ireland. She referred to the current global misconception of what she described as 'the terrorist scenario,' and stated emphatically, "We Muslims do not walk around with guns strapped to our bodies."

From an American viewpoint of Islam and Arab Muslims, Minnesotan David Everson told me his view that, in general, Americans consider Arabs radical; however he, personally, disagrees. "We as Americans need to understand that we should not be judged by gangbangers and thugs in this country and, likewise, we should not judge the Arab Muslim world by its thugs. My understanding is that Arab Muslims are peaceful and have been misjudged for a long time. They need to work hard to distance themselves from terrorists and suicide bombers and, somehow, teach us about their religion."

Rugayah Sharif, Fatima Ali's friend, added, "Sometimes even at the University, professors talk about what Americans think is wrong with Islam. They [Americans] think we are forced to do this or do that because of our religion. We're not. Islam does not force anybody to do anything that they don't want to do. If you are going to do something, it is because you want to, and you believe it is best."

AMERICAN Generalization #2

Islam is a violent religion that preaches death and promotes violence.

Since 9/11 there has been a widespread, almost paranoid belief that Islam is a violent and dangerous religion. Yet a thousand years ago Christians were as fanatic, ruthless, and cruel to each other as they were toward non-believers (heathens). Christianity eventually went through the Reformation and Renaissance, but it took centuries to reach that point. Some wonder if Islam is in the midst of a similar transformation today with the Sunni and Shia infighting in Iraq.

According to a February 2008 opinion piece by the prime minister of Malaysia, Abdullah Ahmad Badawi, in the *Gulf Financial Insider*, identifying Islam and the Muslim world as being synonymous with violence, instability, poverty, illiteracy, injustice, and intolerance is highly misleading.

"Islam has pockets of intolerance, but again that's interpretation," stated Nader Shaheen. "If Islam were a violent religion, people would be opening fire on any given street on any given day. If you are going to terrorize a nation, that's the way to do it. Staying in your house for a week could turn an entire country on its head. But that hasn't happened.

"Americans live under a cloud of fear of another attack on the United States, but I believe the U.S. lives with fear about all kinds of things. Arab Muslim terrorists have not opened up on the streets of America, and it's not because of the Homeland Security Act or because of how diligent police forces are. It's simply that it could not have been the consensus of Islam to make war on the USA.

"So is it fair to say that Islam is a violent religion? No. That comment is a product of information that people have access to; a comment that is utilizing the aspect of fear."

"It's an unfortunate generalization when someone says that Islam is a violent religion that preaches death," said Shaikh Ahmed bin Isa bin Khalifa al Khalifa, assistant undersecretary of Nationality, Passports, and Residence in Bahrain. "You don't see anyone saying that it was the Christians' doing because of the man [Timothy McVeigh] who bombed the Oklahoma Federal building. Nobody condones suicide bombers in any shape or form within the Islamic and Arab world."

Americans watch the Iraq war unfold before them nightly on their televisions. American flags are burned and trampled upon; political leaders are hung in effigy; the Sunnis and Shia are killing each other. Images of these violent outbursts by a minority are what we see on television, which in turn, perpetuates the impression that, yeah, Islam must be a violent religion.

What God would reward anyone for killing innocent women and children? The actions of a militant or suicide bomber are not representative of all Muslims. The Catholic Church has faced its own dark side with priests abusing boys, yet this behavior is not representative of all Catholic priests worldwide.

How then do these radical extremists recruit Muslim men and women to be suicide bombers? Certainly, they must know what the Quran says about suicide.

The answer I heard again and again was that recruitment came through poverty and politics. "I love this question," Rasool Hassan told me point blank. "It is very simple if you think about it. Not everyone is well educated, and not everyone is middle class. If you have a person who does not have food to eat, and his family or he is dying of starvation, and you give him something to eat, he will feel indebted to you. If his knowledge of life is limited, and he is not well educated--and then combine that with being poor--he really has nothing. Imagine that you are a 'good' Muslim explaining to this individual that this is what God wants, and if he does this, this is what he will get. The 'good' Muslim is solving the problems of this poor, uneducated man by offering his food, money, and a house. He promises to keep his family together and safe for the next ten to twenty years. It doesn't take long for this person to begin to believe what he is being told. Once he believes what the 'good' Muslim tells him, he is then under his mercy and will do whatever he is told. It does not matter if it is a man or a woman; if you are underprivileged and uneducated and are offered a way to protect and feed your family, you will believe. Unfortunately, these recruiters are educated and funded in order to have access to money and food to give to those they are recruiting as suicide bombers.

"Then they take it to the next level. You tell this new recruit that he needs to kill people for the cause, including himself. He was raised Muslim, he knows that killing innocent people is wrong. But when these recruiters show this uneducated person movies of children being killed, what do you think this recruit is going to think? I think he will want revenge. They are brainwashed to believe that it doesn't matter if they kill a thousand people in order to get to the targeted person. If I miss you today, I will not miss you tomorrow. This is the biggest problem we are facing with Al Qaeda and other bin Laden groups. And unfortunately, there are people and organizations that financially support these terrorist people."

Nader Shaheen had a slightly different take on the suicide bomber recruitment scenario, saying it is less of a lack of education issue and more about poverty and politics. "The people who are inclined to be suicide bombers are poor, and in many cases, as I understand it, they would be promised $5,000 to $10,000 for their family to be taken care of in return for committing suicide. This is a very large sum of money for someone who is poor. It is in poverty they recruit, and poverty will always reign supreme over one's religious beliefs. You could go to any poor neighborhood in any large city in the United States and find somebody poor, then offer him $10,000 to kill someone. No problem; you will find someone.

"It's not the lack of education; rather, they don't understand how they fit into the world, and they don't have a real sense of self. For example, take the guy who has been working in Detroit for GM for twenty-five years and suddenly loses his job. This man now has identity issues, financial issues, problems with his wife and family, and self-esteem issues. You can very easily recruit from people like that for any cause.

"As I said, it also stems from politics. In order to do away with suicide bombers, you need to ensure there is equitable distribution of wealth. Rich people don't kill themselves. Middle class people rarely go out and kill themselves; it's those in poverty that can be recruited. Even in developing countries, despite poverty, if people live with hope in their lives – it will be better next week; it will be better tomorrow; it will be better in the morning – it is difficult for the suicide recruiters to find sympathetic ears. In general, people aspire, and hope and wish for something better. That's across humanity; it's not just Muslims. These people recruiting suicide bombers are using a much darker and more destructive force and method of using Islam to achieve something political."

Nowhere in the Quran is there an order to kill innocent people, whether Muslim or non-Muslim. Yet we still read about calls for young men to join terrorist groups to travel abroad and wage jihad. Jihad is often misunderstood as meaning a holy war. To wage jihad is to struggle against oppressors and to end oppression, and a second meaning is that jihad is an inner struggle to strive to better oneself. Proponents of Islam reiterate that Islam is the religion of peace, and that the vast majority of Muslims just want to live in peace.

As the Iraq war enters a sixth year and suicide bombings increase, more and more Islamic imams are speaking out with a message that crimes committed in the name of Islam are unacceptable. Enough is enough.

In October 2007, Saudi Arabia's leading religious scholar, Sheikh Abdulaziz Al Sheikh, issued a public statement warning young men in Saudi against traveling abroad "for shameful goals" under the banner of jihad. The Saudi scholar and his council of religious scholars warned that participation with these "outside forces" in a jihad was a violation of Islamic law. It made the Bahrain newspaper, but I could not find it in American newspapers or media; perhaps a condensed version of it was buried on a back page.

Al Qaeda leader Osama bin Laden is from Saudi Arabia, and his militant network recruits heavily there. The majority of the nineteen hijackers who carried out the September 11, 2001 attacks against the United States were from Saudi. The Kingdom of Saudi Arabia has come under international pressure to crack down on religious scholars who preach radical Islam, which in part, prompted the Saudi mufti and his Council of Grand Ulemas, who carry great influence in Sunni circles (the majority religion in the Muslim world), to issue their warning.

Former British Prime Minister Tony Blair on June 4, 2007, had this to say about Islam and terrorism: "The voices of extremism are no more representative of Islam than the use in times gone by of torture to force conversion to Christianity represents the true teaching of Christ."

Perhaps a step further in the right direction is for Muslim countries to break their silence by taking a worldwide public stand to morally condemn violence in the name of Islam. Awareness and education campaigns might gain momentum and such a message might go a long way in presenting the true Islam, dispelling inaccuracies and ignorance commonly shared by Americans and other western countries.

Two years ago when a Danish newspaper published a cartoon of Prophet Muhammad, the ensuing uproar resulted in Danish food bans and riots across the Muslim world. In Bahrain, Danish butter and other products were pulled from restaurants and stores. Although most newspapers in the U.S. did not print the cartoon, it was easily accessible on the Internet. Americans were baffled as to why such a big deal was made over a cartoon. More troubling was that the rioting and deaths portrayed a violent Islam, fueling worldwide flames that this truly must be a violent religion. Meanwhile, Arabs and Muslims protested the fact that non-Muslims were ridiculing their prophet.

Whether or not the cartoon was truly showing disrespect for Muhammad or the Islamic religion, the controversy did raise a question about why representatives of a world religion (Islam) became so emotional that they appeared to lose sight of reality, and portrayed themselves more as loose cannons. Americans have commonly seen caricatures of revered figures in unflattering roles and, although they may disapprove, there are no riots or deaths because of it.

Family is at the core of Islamic teachings. Parents are held accountable before God as to how they raise their children. In return, children are taught to treat their parents with respect. The family lifestyle focuses on helping each other. Furthermore, Muslims are not free to live their lives according to their own desires. They are taught to follow the teachings of the Quran ... but the lines do blur.

› The Arab culture was in existence before Islam. ‹

Maryam al Sheroogi

CHAPTER 2

The Relationship Between Arab Culture and Islam /Islamic Law

Culture and religion are tightly intertwined in the Arab world; one affects the other. If a rule is not written in the Quran, then there is usually a cultural interpretation.

Some examples of this include alcohol consumption, social activities, marriage and engagement customs, censorship, and dress. Determining what is culture and what is religion, and which takes precedent over the other, is a very hot button for Arab Muslims. This is no doubt the one area where most verbal debates center, and opinions wage across the board. For some, the issues are either black or white, while others incorporate the gray areas. But there is no universal agreement among the Bahraini Arabs over many of these topics.

Obviously, with such a hotly contended debate, Americans find themselves completely confused when trying to understand and separate Arab culture from Islamic religion. It just cannot be done.

To Drink or Not to Drink

By law, Bahrain, although a Muslim country, permits Muslims to drink in hotels or homes, but not publicly. If the Quran forbids alcohol, then why does an Islamic government allow it? The easy answer to this question is related to the overwhelming number of non-Muslim expatriates living and working in Bahrain. With their native countries allowing drinking, it would be imprudent and ill-advised to prohibit alcohol consumption, since this country is trying to increase tourism and encourage people to visit and work in Bahrain.

It is illegal, however, for liquor stores to sell alcohol to Arab Muslims. "I believe that Bahrain is the only country in the GCC [Gulf Cooperative Council] that allows drinking everywhere," said Rasool Hassan. "I think drinking may be a good source of income for the government."

Forbidding Muslims to drink is a religious mandate, not a cultural thing, said Shaheen. "What the religion says is: don't be under the influence of anything when you pray. That includes drugs. The point being that if you are going to commune with God, you should do it with a clear head. That's all.

"The first call to prayer is about 4:30 a.m. and the next one is at lunchtime. So if after the last prayer at 4:30 a.m. you get drunk and then sober up by lunchtime, you're okay. But then that's me talking my own book, but it's my understanding. You are not to be under the influence of anything when you pray, and then you are supposed to pray five times a day, which does make it difficult to be under the influence of anything. Having said that, Islam forgives. God is an all-forgiving God. If you do lapse, you will be forgiven."

According to Ms. Fleetwood, "God doesn't use the word 'haram' when forbidding alcohol. He said alcohol has benefits and deterrents. The bad aspect is the effect alcohol has on some people, but then there's also the benefit of alcohol used in medicines and things like that, which God mentions. He said stay away from drinking because the harmful aspects are much worse than any benefits, but it is not absolutely forbidden. It's not written with the word 'haram' (forbidden) in the Quran. Since it is not one hundred percent forbidden, some Muslims drink. Many will see that as God forbidding the bad part, but allowing in measured amounts the good part, which is medicinal. Extremists won't even use mouthwash because it might have alcohol in it.

"The detrimental aspects of drinking, of course, include driving while under the influence, stealing, being physically abusive or committing murder, and in general, just behaving indecently. Just as any other adult, once you drink, you are responsible for your actions. Muslims are never supposed to do anything that can bring harm, unless there is a very good reason."

"I'm a Muslim and since Islam has instructed me not to drink, I don't drink," admitted Hassan. "But personally, I don't see the big deal. Let people drink, but only on one condition – the individual must control himself – and that's a big condition. Unfortunately, you will find families here in Bahrain where the father is always drunk, so we can see the problems drinking can cause society."

ARAB Generalization #1

America has no respect for its women as evidenced by advertisements, movies, TV, and pornography.

It is true that the American culture is obsessed with beauty, being model thin, using cosmetic surgery to look younger—with a push for an endlessly youthful appearance. The reality is that people like to see beautiful people—maybe not necessarily scantily clad—but look at how Americans read everything possible about film stars. Beauty sells movie magazines, no doubt! And yes, objectification of the female body is pervasive in our culture.

On the reverse side, this generalization reflects a very personal choice that really has nothing to do with the United States as a country. If a woman has no respect for herself, she makes many self-destructive choices. If she wants to make X-rated movies; again, that's her choice. And what about the woman who is portrayed as an absolute idiot on television commercials? Can't that be translated as well as a lack of self-respect? Regardless, we would be prudent to refrain from judging others or generalizing about an entire country having no respect for its women.

"These porn movies are not made to please women," a Bahraini woman reminded me. "They are made for men only. So to me it means that women are exploited for the pleasure of men. Furthermore, women from the West are seeking liberation, but they still worry about what men think of them."

The advertising industry has always used sex to sell products, and that practice is certainly not restricted to the States. Arab advertisers do the same thing; the women are more covered up, but they still prance around on television to lure consumers into buying the product. An Arab Muslim man pointed out to me that Egyptian movies have always used women and female beauty to promote films.

American Joan Corey said, "I don't know why it is necessary to portray women scantily dressed. I think here in the States more women are being turned off by that kind of advertising. I have personally stopped at stores and told the management when their advertising was totally inappropriate. I've also told them that if I had children, I would never allow them to shop in their store because of their advertisements."

Maryam al Sheroogi voiced her opinion regarding lack of respect for women: "Arabs ask each other why Americans consider their women cheap. That's somebody's daughter there on TV or in a movie wearing a G-string. But Americans look at the Arabs and say, 'don't you value your women? You just want to hide them, and cover them, and keep them in the house.'"

Michelle LaGue, another American woman, commented. "I understand why the Bahrainis say we have no respect for women, but I feel the Arab Muslim culture has no respect for its women because of the restrictions, such as the clothing, dating, being alone with men, and those kinds of limitations that are placed on them. It's ironic that they would say that about us, when that is the same perception we have of women there."

"It's true that the media and advertisers use women," said Wafaa Ashoor, "But to say America has no respect for its women is not true. I think America respects its women a lot. American women are emotionally stronger than men; they speak up for themselves."

Dr. Mansoor Al Jamri, editor-in-chief of *Alwasat News* supported a similar view: "I think Americans have respect for their women. I think women and the civil rights movement have empowered women in the U.S. in a way that they have some proof of it: Madeleine Albright, Condoleezza Rice, Hillary Clinton, and so on. These women have attained high profile positions.

"I know that Americans are more conservative than Europeans. But in a way, from a Muslim perspective, women are used as a consumer product. Her face and body are used to attract and sell the product, and therefore, lots of films and advertisements show pretty women basically having fun. That attracts money. But that, in itself, whether it is respect or disrespect, is more a difference in perspective. There is a market – and a free market

– from an American point of view. But from a Muslim point of view, there are limits about how far you can use an individual – man or woman – to attract money, because that individual is not a product. The dignity of a person is more important than using him/her as a means to get the money.

"In the Arab world, the Lebanese dominate the advertising industry. Their women are in more than three-fourths of our advertisement industry. They have the pretty women, and their culture of being fun loving, enjoying music and dancing pushes them to show more. We have more than five hundred Arabic TV channels, and only about four of them make a profit. Those are the four that have Lebanese influence. It's Saudi money, but Lebanese programs. The Lebanese are a mix of Christians and Muslims, but I see some hypocrisy in the Arab world with that generalization."

In interviews and articles in the Bahraini newspapers, Bahrainis frequently point to the West, to pornography and the way women dress, as being root causes of rape. However, in truth, since 1993, rape in the U.S. is down seventy-two percent, and other sexual assaults have fallen by sixty-eight percent. Even in the last two years (2005 and 2006) when the FBI reported a rise in violent crime, the number of rapes continued to fall. If pornography causes widespread rape in the United States, then why are sexual assaults on a decline in this country? With the widespread and well-publicized commitment to prosecute offenders and educate the American public about rape, there is no reason to believe that sexual assault reports are underreported, as they were in the 1980s and earlier.

ARAB Generalization #2

The American culture has destroyed the family system/family values, and they [Americans] have no morals.

The majority of American women I spoke with agreed that there are definitely segments of our society that have destroyed family values. One such segment is within the African American population where many fathers are absent, and many women raise their children alone. Whether or not Bahraini Muslims base this generalization totally on statistics within the African American segment of American society is unknown.

"When someone grows up seeing that, of course, they think it's the norm," said Joan Corey. "I hope they [Bahrainis] are not basing their opinions on what they see on American television sitcoms and shows. That's about as far from reality as you can get."

"This is what we see in your media," Salah al Shuroogi admitted. "Here, from the first year of birth, children are encouraged to be connected to the family. I don't see the United States as a country promoting that."

"We are raised to show respect to the elderly," adds his twenty-one-year-old daughter, Fatima. "When I have children, I will teach them the importance of visiting my father and mother. I visit my grandmother in Saudi Arabia every three weeks or so. In our culture, when I see my father, I come to him and hug him, then kiss him on the forehead to show respect. In your culture, you would never see a twenty-one-year-old do that, and then sit and talk to his father. Your media, or at least what we see on television, shows no feelings between family members."

Sandy Meyer, another American interviewed, partially agreed with the generalization, particularly as it relates to abortion. "Countries can't understand how abortion can be legal here—where we are killing our own babies, and we have such high abortion rates. In their culture, they get married just to have babies. So I understand their point of view."

"I think that perception of immorality and lost family values is everywhere in the world though, not just in America," interjected Corey. "It's what's shown on TV. We ourselves even have perceptions of people who live in Boston or on the West Coast, for example, as having weaker family values than we have in the Midwest."

"The people who are shooting each other in the streets of America are the ones who are giving us the bad name," asserted Jayne Dietz. "And that's what you hear about in the media — sex offending teachers, school shootings, street killings, or athletes on drugs/steroids."

Bahraini Wafaa Ashoor disagreed with the above generalization. "I think everybody has destroyed everyone's values; we can't blame America for everything."

Family Values

Families are fractionalized today, but is that true only in America? I think it extends to the entire Western world and beyond. Having spent a fair amount of time in Bahrain, I know they are not immune either. Drugs, violence, rape, crime, and prostitution – all immoral activities – are no longer isolated occurrences in Bahrain. These soaring issues impacting the fabric of society cannot be blamed only on Asians and other expatriates. This is a sad reality that Bahrainis are struggling to accept.

The world is changing so fast that families are pulled in different directions, and many are losing sight of their real values. Our world has truly become a global village of diverse cultures that influence everyone. This is not a problem associated only with the West.

One hundred years ago cultures were isolated. Coming into contact with someone who had different ideas and beliefs was more of a culture shock. People today can better identify with another culture's ideas and beliefs, and are much more accepting of each other. Being of a different religion or culture is less likely to separate people.

Within the Bahraini Arab culture there is some apprehension about this global village of cultural modernism. They are joining it, but on their own terms, and in a cultural and moral context of what is meaningful to the Arab culture. Agree or not, modernism is a part of life. This fear of modernism causes some individuals to cling more strongly to family relationships and old-fashioned values, while others shift away. But adapting to a changing world society does not mean abandoning heritage or cultural traditions and values, nor does it mean being swept off one's feet by unabashed liberalism. Family will and should always be important, and families will always have a crucial role in preparing future generations.

Twenty-one-year-old Nofa Ghanim al Sulaiti agreed that Arab family values are being affected. She blamed it on television, peer pressure, and even education. "Kids see a lot of things on TV. They won't understand it until they ask their parents if it's cool to do this; is it okay to say that?

If his friends smoke, he may start smoking. Why shouldn't he? He sees smoking portrayed as cool on TV. Sometimes kids don't care what their parents think.

"A lot of foreign teachers come to Bahrain to teach our children. They might teach them things they are not supposed to. For example, in America it is okay to go out. But in the Bahraini home you are taught that it's not okay. So here the morals are being challenged and changing.

"Reputation is another important factor. Although as teens and young adults, Americans can go just about anywhere they want, that is especially difficult for Arabs. For example," Nofa emphasized, "Bahrainis know by a family name if you are Shia or Sunni. If people know my name is al Sulaiti, they know I am Sunni; they have access to information about me, who is my grandfather, who is my father, where I was born, where my parents' house is, where my great-grandfather came from. In the Arab world, it is an honor to have your family name. So we must be careful with it. It's like a reputation that is almost more than that – it's a religion."

Nofa feels that the importance of reputation is part of the reason why an unmarried woman would never move out of her parents' house and share a flat with another girlfriend. "It's not that its haram [forbidden], but it would be difficult. It's that reputation thing again. If a girl moves out and is not married, a man will wonder about her reputation and why she has moved out. He is going to think it must be bad in her house and something unacceptable is happening. People start talking. If you have a good, specific reason to move out from your parents' house, then it's okay. But if you don't, people will talk, and you will get a bad reputation. Reputation is a very, very big thing in the Arab world, and it's always been like that. I can't say if other girls my age agree with this philosophy or not, but we live with it. A girl is Arab reputation for the whole family. If something goes wrong for this girl, her family will be shamed."

Nofa's mother, Naseem al Noaime, explained how people also talked when she was a young adult. "When I finished high school, I wanted to go to the university to learn English. But in 1970, Bahrain did not have any universities; we went to Egypt, Lebanon, or Kuwait. People came up to my father and asked him how he could send his daughter alone to a foreign country. At that time, it was a very big thing and not the norm, like today, to go abroad for your education. People told him that because I was not married and because of our family name alone, that he should not allow it. But my father disagreed; he also wanted me to learn English."

Twenty-two-year-old Rugayah Sharif talked about school friends at her university: "They are so innocent about life. They have been sheltered. When they are going to watch a movie at home, their families sit with them. Their parents monitor every thing they do."

Rasool Hassan outlined a scenario he thought was applicable to Bahrain's growing problem of juvenile delinquency. "It goes back to the cultural family. In Bahrain you will find a father with a large family to support. He works from morning to night for a relatively low salary. He comes home exhausted and just wants to eat, and then to be left alone to sleep. His children's needs are not being met. We have undereducated and jobless people here; we are not all college educated, driving BMWs."

With no one at home to pay attention to the children, the children will find others who will, and worse yet, they will often seek out negative attention — stories about which find their way into the newspapers daily. It is so important for parents to teach their children right from wrong during the crucial formative years. Children learn from their role models who, hopefully, are their parents. They need parental guidance, rules, accountability, and consequences. Does Bahrain's Muslim society rely too much on, and deem it okay to have their children cared for and "raised" by inexperienced foreign maids as glorified babysitters?

The Midwestern American contributors I spoke with found it very interesting that it is normal for Bahraini families to employ live-in maids, and that these maids earned such low salaries for what they are expected to do. "It cuts across all culture lines," commented Michelle LaGue. "Interesting that they are going to have someone clean and cook for them who is considered lesser, but to have these maids, who are probably very uneducated and unfamiliar with the Arab culture and society, care for their children; I find that very, very interesting."

Rasool Hassan, the father of two young boys and an infant girl, tries hard to talk to and understand his sons. He wants his family to be close. "We are not only father and sons, but also friends. I do not want my sons to feel shamed if they ask me an unwanted question. When I was a boy, we thought of things that we could not, or felt we could not, talk to our parents about or ask them questions about. I want an atmosphere where my children are comfortable asking me any questions."

A Bahraini woman, who wished to remain anonymous, told me that the real solution to the problem of declining family values "is to raise today's children with strong moral values and a strong sense of being able to distinguish between right and wrong, so they can protect themselves from harm. Of course, it is not humanly possible to monitor or supervise all the activities of every child, whether they are on the computer, out playing with their friends, in school, listening to music, or watching movie videos on TV. It's a fact that today's children worldwide are exposed to high levels of both positive and negative information as a direct result of the Internet and media.

"Moral and value-based education is required in our present times whereby our children are able to analyze any information or action as good and bad, learn and accept the good and discard the bad. The forbidden fruit is always tempting. When we equip our children with strong moral education and guidance, only then will they find it easy to hold themselves in the face of any temptations and pressures, which may come their way as they grow up."

"Instilling 'proper' Islamic values, and seeing that they are properly practiced, is the job of parents and should be taught from the moment of birth," according to Lee Ann Fleetwood, although she admits that the schools, to some degree, have a responsibility for ensuring that a moral atmosphere prevails. "If children are properly raised with Islamic values at home, they wouldn't have to be forced on them at school.

"America is a huge melting pot of cultures, so you have your Americans that keep family traditions the same way as Bahrainis, and then you have Americans that scatter as soon as they turn eighteen. It depends on how you were raised," asserted Fleetwood.

The *Bahrain Tribune* carried a story in its July 4, 2007, edition about the Bahrain Women's Society and the launch of their Personal Freedom Act. The article states that the act was intended as part of an effort to encourage people to rebel against unrealistic traditions and lifestyles that prevent most Arabs from achieving their dreams. The act stressed that old-fashioned education, restricted family principles, outdated legislation, the absence of contemporary religious dialogue, weak non-governmental organizations, and poor media are key factors challenging human development in the Arab world. Dr. Wajiha Al Baharna, the Society president was quoted: "We have chosen personal freedom because such a concept is missing among Arabs, and any reforms should start from inside to outside and not the opposite... To have complete freedoms, we need to free ourselves from our fear, self-rejection, and doubts."

The article goes on to say that this act was launched to save the new generation from making mistakes made by the older ones, and encourage youth to feel free to explore the world and reach their full potential for happiness. Specifically, the act calls for better child rearing, encouraging families to abandon the practice of controlling their children out of fear, and instead promoting them to be happy and self-confident. It also stresses major changes in school curricula, "especially the outdated teaching methods by which teachers pass on the new information to students and not promote them to search for knowledge."

In theory, family values remain important as part of the Bahraini Arab culture and religion. Arab tradition strives to maintain the extended family. Because a man is expected to be the breadwinner, he is required to clothe, house and feed his family, and any relatives who require similar support. A man should look after his mother, father, younger brothers, and unmarried sisters, plus cousins, aunts and uncles who need help or shelter. It is common for Arabs to care for their parents until they die. Nursing homes and assisted-living facilities, which are prevalent in the United States, are virtually unheard of in the Arab Muslim world, as they go against the deeply entrenched cultural practice of living with one's parents after marriage.

Rasool Hassan explained, "We grow up with families and parents, and we don't leave them unless we choose to build our own home or walk away from them. We don't usually give them a choice as to whether they are willing to stay in their home or come live with us. If they are willing to stay in the family house and still have children at home, we go and visit them weekly. Every Saturday I have lunch or dinner with my parents."

Hameed Alawi echoed a similar view. "I totally agree that family values are being destroyed in America, although I also believe that most Americans have good families. Maybe that I see this differently comes from my having lived and worked with Americans. I also agree that American morals are not what they probably once were. Here we have big families and we eat together. For example, my older brother is married, and he and his wife live above us on the second floor, but he is still living with us. Even when people are married here they are still living with family. We communicate with them constantly and consult them when faced with big issues. Once I had my master's degree and began working, I was able to help them out financially even though I was not expected to."

Fatima Ali also agreed. "In our culture, we visit home on a daily basis at least for three to four hours. Here in Bahrain everyone lives close by; the farthest you might be from your parents is half an hour."

"Don't you think eighteen is a dangerous age for someone to go out on their own? To work, live alone or share a flat with someone? You must be mature to do that," commented Salah al Shuroogi. "Maybe if young Americans stayed living with their families until they were older, it would help reduce crime and drug use. By staying with the family, everyone remains connected and communication stays open. They can see family closeness."

ARAB Generalization #3

Western culture is very lax regarding women's clothing that gives mixed messages to men.

The Americans interviewed overwhelmingly agreed with this generalization Ironically, some Bahraini men disagreed with it.

Nader Shaheen, who characterized this statement as "horribly sweeping," offered his opinion. "I think again it's a personal choice that is consciously made. In social and casual settings, clothing can be more revealing but, by and large, businesswomen, doctors, and women in the workplace do not dress that way. I doubt American women are going to church in bikinis or turning up for a business meeting in a short skirt and midriff top."

Media Violence

In the United States there has been intense public focus on the impact of violence, sex, and adult language used on television, the Internet, in music lyrics, video games, and movies. A highly charged debate began in April 2007 when the Federal Communications Commission (FCC) issued a report to Congress saying lawmakers could regulate television violence without violating the First Amendment's free speech protections.

The *Associated Press* carried a story in American newspapers in June 2007 about parents opposed to media violence and sex. The non-partisan Kaiser Family Foundation conducted a survey among one thousand eight randomly selected parents of children aged two to seventeen as to whether parents or the government should limit kids' access to TV programs. Overall results indicated that two-thirds of parents are very concerned about their children's exposure to media sex and violence, with television and the Internet as the most frequently cited sources of concern. The results also showed that parents would give "broad support" for new federal limits on such material shown on television. Two of three parents surveyed felt they were already closely tracking their children's TV and Internet exposure along with video game playing.

Respondents reported the belief that parents, teachers, and friends have far more influence over children than the media. "Parents are fooling themselves if they believe they have that much control," an un-named expert on the effect the media have on children said during a panel discussion that accompanied the release of the poll and report. The Kaiser report also found that one in four parents felt the media was mainly a negative influence on their children; about a third said the media are mainly positive; and slightly more than that said the media have little impact on their children. Half of the respondents indicated that they were very concerned that their children see too much violence and sexual material. This number was down from more than six in ten who expressed those same worries in a 1998 Kaiser survey. Black and Hispanic parents were more likely than whites to voice that concern, according to the *Associated Press* article.

Recent polls have found that, across age demographics, most Bahrainis spend their free time at the shopping malls and cinemas. Many Americans are unaware that movies and DVDs are censored in Bahrain, except for the ample illegally purchased DVDs on the street. With satellite TV so popular and accessible, it's also easy to view uncensored movies and pornography.

The Ministry of Information has a team of people who watch movies. Based on a set of standards, they request certain parts removed, such as nudity and profanity, before movies are shown in the Bahrain cinemas. Hameed Alawi, who was living in the UK when the movie *Titanic* was released, saw it there and then again in Bahrain. He said the "sanitized" Bahraini version had deleted the scene where Leonardo DiCaprio sketched the picture of the naked Rose, played by Kate Winslet.

Some parents in Bahrain forbid their kids to go to movies altogether. "For example," explained Maryam al Sheroogi, "one of my brothers doesn't allow his kids to go to the cinema. He thinks movies are a bad influence. I enjoy going to the cinema. It is not against our culture; it will not change us."

"Since you can download music from the Internet and other places, it wouldn't make sense for Bahrain to try to censor music CDs," explained Fatima Ali. "We get the same music as you get in the U.S. or UK. It becomes a matter of personal conviction as to whether or not you listen to songs with suggestive lyrics or profanity. I usually argue with my cousin about the music he listens to. I tell him if the songs involve bad language or are demeaning to women, then he should not be listening to them."

Recognizing youth worldwide as a crucial media target market, MTV Arabia debuted in Bahrain in November 2007. MTV in the United States, known for airing provocative videos of scantily clad women, has a sanitized

Middle East version. Abdullatif Al Sayegh, chief executive of Arab Media Group, which along with MTV Networks International owns MTV Arabia, explained that the Arabic channel has "culturally sensitive editors going through content of the programming". MTV Arabia hopes to set itself apart from other satellite music channels saturating the Middle East market by emphasizing local music talent (forty percent of its content) and programs aimed at addressing the concerns of Arab youth. It will feature sixty percent international music (hip hop and R&B) and local adaptations of MTV's popular non-music shows, including reality television.

"We hope to provide a platform for Arab youth to break boundaries without disrespecting their tradition and culture," stated Bhavneet Singh, managing director of the Emerging Markets Group, part of MTV Networks International.

› Traditionally, the Bahraini marriage ceremony centered on the pearl, Bahrain's primary economical resource until the discovery of oil in 1932. The groom decorated a plain wooden chest with carved brass and filled it with pearls specially gathered for his bride. The diver's chest, originally used for storing his catch, was given in marriage to his bride. The pearl was associated with fertility. ‹

CHAPTER 3

The Relationship Between Socializing and Marriage Within the Arab Culture

The relationship between marriage, engagement, and socialization among the sexes is extremely complex and difficult to grasp for Americans unfamiliar with the Arab culture. Most of my information came from interviews with young, unmarried Bahraini adults aged twenty to twenty-seven.

Islam gives women the right to choose their husbands, yet Arab Muslims often do not. The Arab culture allows for "arranged" engagements and marriages whereby a couple is "sponsored" and then introduced to each other. Only then can a woman decide if this particular suitor is someone she wishes to spend the rest of her life with.

Hameed, twenty-seven, admitted he's a bit late for the average Bahraini male to marry. The maximum age, he said, is usually twenty-five or twenty-six. He's still single for the simple reason that he had been completing his master's degree, and financially it would have been very difficult to be married and also remain committed to his educational goals.

Shia siblings Fatima and Naeema Ali and Fatima's girlfriend, Rugayah, all in their early twenties, enjoy shopping, coffee breaks, lunching with girlfriends, going to movies, working out at the gym, and visiting friends at their homes, which is probably their more common social activity. According to the three women, the usual marriage age for Bahraini girls starts at seventeen and goes up to twenty or twenty-two, then, similar to a graph, it declines until age thirty. A woman not married by age thirty, is considered "expired and on the shelf." The three agreed that the cultural age expectations should not be the guiding rule; after all, a woman may feel very young at thirty and/or she may have very good reasons for not becoming engaged until that age."

Naeema and Rugayah are still in college and single, as is Fatima, a recent college graduate. They wasted no time explaining the many cultural restrictions placed upon them.

"While at the university, it is okay for a girl to have coffee with a guy if he asks her," Rugayah said. "But if she were to go out with him after studying or after work, people would ask questions and start nasty rumors."

Fatima and Naeema nodded their heads simultaneously in agreement before Fatima added, "The three of us would find that normal, but the extremists would not, so there is a restriction on where, how, and when for Arab girls."

This restriction comes from the culture, not the religion, the girls told me. "Society abuses this thing," said Rugayah. "Sometimes the parents are open minded and say the young people are free to do what they want. But the way our society treats girls who go out with guys they are not related to... well, this is the problem. Of course, we can't have boyfriends and girlfriends. We're not supposed to go out with guys unless we are engaged."

"A couple holding hands in public is okay, but a guy putting his arm around a girl — that's not a restriction, that's a definite no-no. And of course, there won't be any kissing in public," Fatima warned.

Nader Shaheen added, "There is a secular law that says public displays of affection are prohibited, but that usually means being all over each other. And frankly, they should go get a room. Bahrain is conservative, and this certainly is not California."

Bahrain's Arab culture and attitudes appear much more open and free as recently as one to two generations ago as opposed to the situation today. "When my mom was younger than me," reported twenty-two-year-old Rugayah, "she and her friends used to wear miniskirts and do whatever they wanted. Life was different then; it was much less restrictive. They all lived in small, nearby villages and knew each other. My mother said they were even allowed to play with boys.

"Even when we were kids," she continued, "We played innocently. Kids nowadays have it different, even the programs they watch. They've got mobile phones, the computer, and email. It's all different today, and all because of the media they're exposed to."

In the 1960s and '70s it was commonplace for women in Bahrain to wear short dresses and miniskirts. As Sunni Wafaa Ashoor recalled, "We wore miniskirts back then. I still remember my mother wearing a micro-skirt. She had long, dyed-blonde hair. Being raised with Americans, she wanted to look like them. We were raised in Saudi Arabia at Aramco (Saudi Arabian Oil Company), now known as Saudi Aramco. [Aramco is actually a separately enclosed city where the oil company is located.] She and I both wore bikinis on the beach in Saudi. I danced in front of men, swam in the water, and lay on the beach with boys; I didn't care. It was not frowned upon.

"In the '70s, only the Shia wore hijab, and practically nobody in Bahrain wore it. When I was young, we were allowed to play outside with boys; my mother did not mind. It was more open, especially living in Aramco; you could do whatever you wanted. But back in the '70s, there were no problems with men. Their minds were open, innocent, and pure. The modernization changed all that; it's everywhere. Life can never go back to that of the '70s."

"When the '80s came, we opened our eyes," interjected Maryam al Sheroogi. "Because of the Wahhabis[1] and their extreme views. They were strong in Saudi and came to Bahrain and Kuwait, and opened our minds about things we didn't know about. We feel that we are in the middle; we don't feel that we are extreme. My friend's mother is almost forty-three, but she is very extreme. She wears three pairs of socks; she doesn't want anyone to see her ankles."

Mrs. Ashoor recalls people beginning to discuss clothing and hijab in the '80s, partly because it was being talked about on Bahraini television. "Before then, television only had shows on, but then they began to speak about women

[1]Wahhabis (followers of Abd al-Wahhab (1703-92), who stringently opposed all practices not sanctioned by the Quran. The Wahhabis, founded in the eighteenth century, are the most conservative Muslim group, today found mainly in Saudi Arabia.

needing to wear hijab and other clothing views. They never said 'put this on and wear it,' rather, they said 'this is in the Book' [Quran]. They made us aware of it. Sometimes the imam spoke about how we should wear hijab, and how men and women should behave," continued Mrs. Ashoor. "And then there is the culture. Many ladies in Bahrain took the hijab, but later in the '80s began removing it once they were in the privacy of their homes."

Fatima Senan, a Sunni woman who has known Wafaa since their university days in Kuwait, wears not only niqab (face veil), but also black gloves and the shapeless, traditional one piece black abaya (defa), said wearing hijab began in late 1980 and continued through 1981. "By 1982 most Bahraini women were wearing hijab. While I was married, I only wore hijab. When my husband died, I thought it better to wear niqab, which is when I started wearing this." She pointed to the veil covering her entire face except for the eyes.

Wafaa added, "There is a sentence in the Book about hijab. When I read it, I think it means wearing hijab is enough. But when Fatima reads it, she interprets it as 'no, hijab is not enough.' And her interpretation is not wrong; we are both right."

"Back when my mother was young, they had extended family with cousins nearby. Your neighbor was usually a cousin, who in our culture we can marry," pointed out Fatima Ali. "There is more religious awareness now about Islam; how to dress like a Muslim, and how to act like a Muslim. Twenty to fifty years ago there wasn't this restriction. Our parents were taught what was right or wrong, and it was up to them to act accordingly. In our culture today, a male non-relative would never be allowed to roam the house with a Bahraini woman there alone. And some of the stricter Muslim families here still insist upon you marrying your cousin."

"In Bahrain it seems to go in thirty- or forty-year cycles where the culture will be really strict about something, then become more relaxed," said Maryam al Sheroogi. "I think it depends on the religious leaders at the time. They are very important, and we are listening to them. If they become extreme in their views, we will become extreme. They open our eyes to issues that were once closed. It's the same as wearing hijab. We didn't know about it until the Wahhabis came and told us."

Culturally Engaged, but Legally Married

If there is no dating in this Arab culture, how can someone become engaged to someone they know nothing about?

"Sometimes they [engagements] are arranged by families," began Rugayah, a Shia. "If a guy wants to meet me, he might call my aunt and tell her this. The only reason a girl would agree to meet a guy is because she is looking to settle down and get married; otherwise, she would just say she is not interested. It's not as common now," she continued, "But sometimes if a guy sees a girl he wants to meet, he goes directly to her family. They talk and sometimes the parents agree that they can talk on the phone. If they both agree that they want to get to know each other more, they get engaged."

Fatima Ali tried to clarify, saying, "In our culture, engagement does not necessarily lead to marriage. You're engaged and then you're not. An engagement is just a time period where you get to know someone better. It can be for six months, one year, even three years, and then there is the marriage. It would be scary to marry someone you did not know. It's also okay to break off the engagement; there's no stigma attached to doing that."

Rugayah outlined the events leading up to an engagement for Shia girls: "When my aunt came to me about this guy, she said 'I have this person who wants to meet you, and I have nominated you,' which is the wording used. What she is really saying is to be happy about this. If the person who 'found' the guy thinks he's a good person, and if you are looking to settle down, then you agree to meet. Prior to the first meeting, you ask for details about him, the neighborhood he grew up in, who his family is, is he a good or bad guy. You don't just meet anybody."

An interview is scheduled at the girl's home for the two to ask questions of each other. "He does not talk to the parents," Fatima added, "Because we are making the choice, not our parents. At the first interview you just look for the click -- that look the two of you give each other. If it's not there and still not there at the second interview, you can cancel him out and not see him again. You want honest answers and honest questions. Is he a person you can trust and want to spend the rest of your life with?

"Some guys regard the engagement period as a time to let the girl dress and do whatever she wants, then he shows his true colors later. That's why it's so important to ask questions at the interview. 'I'm not going to wear a scarf, is that okay with you?' If he says no, then you know where you stand. The interview is when you find out as much about him as you can through your questions. He also asks you questions. Find out his hobbies, what he does in his spare time, how he feels about the things you have strong opinions about.

"If I like this guy and he likes me, we agree to get engaged," Fatima said. "Then he meets the immediate family, and they go through the fine details before they settle on a mahar [dowry]. They agree how much it will be, when is the best time to get the malcha [contract], give the mahar, and have the celebration. It's all about where, when, and how. Along with the contract comes an engagement ring, except that we don't just get the ring; we get the whole lot."

The "whole lot" [which is exactly how it is referred to] consists of diamond necklace, earrings, ring and bracelet – a set that the couple sometimes picks out together. Sets are visibly displayed in every jewelry store. "When a man becomes engaged, he wants the woman to believe he is generous and making a good impression on her," said Rugayah.

In the past there was no marriage contract, according to Hameed Alawi, only an oral agreement. The woman said she would be his wife and the man accepted it, and that was it. Eventually issues arose, mainly government-related, and the Kingdom initiated the written contract and marriage agreement. "There must be written agreements now to be legal so you can prove you are married. These are necessary to show if you want to buy a house, for example. The government marriage is the customary one that is now recognized worldwide. The second one, called Zwaj Al-Motaa, is the contract both sign, which is the temporary marriage that can last one day, one month, or one year."

Once the contract is signed, the couple is legally married and culturally engaged, although the Zwaj Al-Motaa is not widely accepted as legal, according to some of the Sunni Muslims interviewed.

"The Prophet Muhammad instituted the Zwaj Al-Motaa for a few reasons," continued Hameed, "But mainly because of the wars. There were a lot of men killed and wives left widowed with no one to support them. They would then be lost in society," explained the young Shia man. "This is one of the reasons why God permits Muslims to marry four wives. Another reason for the Zwaj Al-Motaa is for a woman who reaches the age of thirty or more and has not been proposed to yet--which in our culture at that age she is considered on the shelf [unmarriageable]. Because adultery and having sex without being married is against Islam, divorced women are included in the Zwaj Al-Motaa, thus allowing them to have sexual relations. Of course, there are those who abuse Zwaj Al-Motaa. Some men want to have the temporary marriage just so they can sleep with a woman and then break up with her later."

Wafaa Ashoor elaborated upon the cultural practice that Sunnis follow regarding introduction and engagement. Similar to the Shia, if the girl is not ready for or interested in marriage, she would not want to meet a boy. "She can say 'hi, how are you' to boys at the university, but nothing more than that. She will not make a relationship unless she is willing to get married. It is fine to go to a coffee shop as part of a mixed group, but if anyone saw her alone with a boy, they would talk or call the girl's mother.

"Let's say a boy meets a girl at the university or someplace and wants to marry her. With Sunnis, it's between the families and the lady first," emphasized Wafaa. "The boy tells his mother that he wants to marry the girl, and he and his mother sit and discuss it. If the mother knows the girl's family and knows that it is a good family, she arranges a meeting with the girl's mother and goes for coffee at her home. The boy's mother brings along his sisters to the meeting at the girl's house. She tells the girl's mother that she is there to ask for the hand of her daughter for her son. If the girl's mother agrees, the next step is for the boy's father to visit the girl's father.

"It is important for each family to know that the other family is a good family," Wafaa stressed. Similar to the Shia tradition, the couple interviews each other, discusses important issues, and determines where they agree and disagree."

"An important issue they discuss is if the girl is willing to live with the boy's family," added Fatima Senan. "Many boys can't afford to start their future with a minimal salary living on their own. Many fathers provide their sons a room on the second floor of their house. Many Sunni girls will agree to the marriage, but only on the condition that they live alone, and not with his family."

"I never met my husband, had never seen him," disclosed Wafaa, "But my uncle knew him. One day he saw my uncle and casually mentioned that he was looking for the right girl to marry. My uncle told him about me. Once I agreed to meet, my uncle made a meeting in his office. My prospective husband seemed to be a very nice young man, so we continued talking on the phone (with permission from my mother), but did not see each other.

"About ten days later, he came to the house with my uncle to meet my mother and have a cup of tea. We talked on the phone for another ten days, and then he said he would send his mother to my house. She came with her daughters and told my mother that she would like me as her son's wife. I agreed since I knew him and was happy with him.

"It could be that just the mother came or maybe the mother and one of the boys' sisters, but the more women who come, the more respect. If the mother goes alone, the girl's family might wonder what kind of family is this that none of the other women and girls come along. Even the aunties come. It's a good way to show off his side of the family; saying that all the family wants you. It shows strength. If just the mother and maybe one of her daughters came, the girl's mother might think that this family might not have a close bond with each other. Even the man will come with his uncles, brothers, and brothers-in-law. It shows that they love him. But if he comes alone, it indicates a separated family that is not very cohesive.

"My husband was mature enough to discuss all issues openly, which allowed me to tell him everything also, so I was okay and knew we were ready to marry. After his mother came to our house with his three sisters, we decided when to do the melcha [also spelled malcha]. Since my father had died, my husband spoke to my grandfather who was looking after me. They decided on the phone to meet at my grandfather's house for the signing. Some people go to the mosque for the malcha signing, as you need the shaikh. Some ask the shaikh to come to their house; it's whatever is convenient for the men.

"A few days before the signing, we buy the whole lot – the gold and bling things! We did not pick out ours together. He picked out six sets that he liked and brought them to my home. But not everyone does it that way. My husband happened to know someone at a gold shop who trusted him and let him bring the sets. I selected the set that I liked, and he returned the others. Then we had the rings engraved."

Fatima Senan went alone to buy her set, which is not unusual for Sunni girls, she pointed out. "Men mostly think it is a girl thing. They tell her what the budget is and to buy whatever she wants."

"My brother-in-law, for example, gave his wife just a ring, but it was very expensive," added Wafaa. "So it depends, although it usually is a set. It's not something you wear every day either, because it is so expensive and elaborate; you usually just wear the jewelry to weddings or parties."

The Malcha

The signing of the contract [malcha/melcha] is the guarantee for both individuals that their wishes will be adhered to during their engagement. Since they have completed the interviews and openly discussed the issues of clothing, working, having children, and other important topics, there should be no surprises on the day the contract is signed. This practice holds true for both Shia and Sunni.

Fatima and Rugayah explained the Shia contract. If the boy writes down that he does not want the girl to work or he expects her to wear an abaya, and he knew from the interviews that she did not agree, she will not sign the contract. This was the entire point of the interviews. When the shaikh comes to the designated Shia location [usually a hotel, but it could be the woman's home] with the contract, he asks each one what the rules are and writes them down, after which they both sign. Sometimes the two are in separate rooms while the contract is negotiated, and other times they are together; it depends on the couple. If they are in separate rooms, one person signs and then the shaikh takes the document to the room where the other individual then signs it.

"If after the marriage the man wants her to quit working, the woman has the signed contract as proof that he agreed that she would continue working; thus, he cannot make her quit," stated Rugayah.

"The imam will ask the lady if there is anything influencing her answer," added Fatima Ali, "Because if she is being forced to agree to something, they cannot be married. He asks her seven times; repeating this same question seven times." Once both parties have signed the contract, a traditional ceremony occurs, at least for the Shia. According to Fatima, there must be a ceremony, even if only a small one.

Because Wafaa's future father-in-law was paralyzed, he sent his sons to Wafaa's grandfather's house for their malcha signing. The Sunni ritual differs slightly from the Shia practice. "The men are in one room and the women in another, but we can hear what is going on," Wafaa said, recalling her marriage day. "The shaikh brought the paper and asked my husband if he would like to marry me, to which he said yes. Next, the shaikh sent my uncle to my room. I came to the door and he said, 'do you want to take him as your husband?' and I said 'yes.' There should be two witnesses there, which is to prevent something happening, like if I said 'no,' and then he went back to the men's room and told the shaikh that I said 'yes.' So there were two men standing behind my uncle when he asked me. He must hear the word 'yes' – which indicates acceptance. He then went back to the shaikh and told him that he heard 'yes.' In our culture, a woman is not allowed to go before the men and agree to the marriage. I had sponsored my grandfather to speak on my behalf, which is why I was not in the room. I believe it should be this way. We don't like the mixing of sexes much, especially on these occasions."

The reason for this separation of sexes, according to Wafaa, is partly as an assurance in the event that one of the boys or men present is not "good." "At the gathering, many men are there, not only the family," she explained. "There might also be friends of the couple. We don't always know each other. Maybe a boy would look at a girl in a bad way – not a respectful way – so we believe it is better to not mix.

"After everyone had signed the contract, my husband came to me in the room where I was sitting with ladies of my family. Before this time, he was not allowed to touch or kiss me. At this point, all of the family men (my husband, uncles, and grandfather) can come into the room. Only those who live in the house can sit with us, which is why we are not wearing hijab. From now on, he and I are together."

Wafaa laughed as her memory retraced the events of that day twenty-five years before. "My first thought as he entered the room was whether he would recognize me, because we do look different with our hair showing and makeup on. He was so excited as he came in, saying hello to everyone. Then he looked at me with the expression, 'I know you from somewhere'. He didn't recognize me!

"That is when he put the set of jewelry on me, which is symbolic for 'you are my wife; this is a gift for you'. Then we took pictures. I was then officially married. Afterwards we went out to eat.

"My mother and I had done my hair up at home, and I was wearing a pretty pink dress that she had made. For malcha, the Sunni girls can wear any type and color of dress they want. We have no type of symbolic arrangements, rituals, or special clothing like the Shia."

Fatima Ali described the Shia jalwa [ceremony], which usually takes place in a hotel and extends over three days elsewhere. "At this point, the guy has never seen the woman without her scarf; he's never touched her or even held her hand. After the contract is signed – the first day of the celebration – she comes in wearing a beautiful green veil with embroidery that is covering her entire face. [Green signifies purity and life, which is why the veil is green.] He leads her to a chair where once sitting, he begins to place seven veils on her head in layers. The man pulls them back and kisses her forehead signifying that she is a treasure and not a trophy. She has been made up very nicely and her hair is done. From then on, she does not wear the scarf in front of him when they are at home. Sometimes guests in attendance will hold lit candles. The man offers the woman a piece of food, they kiss, and then rose water and saffron are placed on her. Following this is a huge banquet."

The second evening of celebration is for the women, and is the traditional henna night. Henna signifies happiness, eternal love, youthfulness, and long life, and the henna plant has been used in beauty rituals and ceremonies for centuries. It is the oldest documented cosmetic and an ancient art of body decoration. The girls said it takes about two hours to apply and another four hours to dry. Henna stays on for weeks. In Bahrain the choice of henna is either black or brownish red, with the latter being the most popular shade.

The third evening is the engagement night, which is also only for women. It is usually held in someone's home. Early that morning the bride goes to the salon to have makeup applied. The man has purchased the wedding rings and with her name engraved on her ring along with the date. She has done the same with his wedding band. In Bahrain, women wear gold or silver jewelry, but men wear only silver.

Fatima explained that some couples don't want a celebration for the jalwa or to do the henna, so they have only the wedding party. Others have a small engagement party and a lavish wedding party or vice versa. Only the family is allowed to take photographs of the couple, because outsiders might take photos of the women without their scarves or put the photos on the Internet.

Hameed offered a Shia male perspective to the engagement process: "In the Islam religion, when you want to marry a woman, the *religion* allows you to see her hair and part of her body. However, the Arab culture does not allow that. In Bahrain the *culture* ranks higher than the Islamic rule."

He admitted though that today there are men and women who date behind their parents' backs, though he personally believes they should be engaged first so they can go out together in public.

Legally Married

There is Arab culture, and there is the Islamic way. According to the Islamic way, Wafaa is legally married after completing the events she described earlier. Culturally, however, a couple must announce the marriage. She explained, "Once you have announced it, you can touch each other and be alone in a room together. The way it is usually announced for Sunnis is with a wedding party, but you can also announce it in the newspaper. We just put our picture in the newspaper and went on a honeymoon. If you 'make a wedding,' then everybody will know right away. There is also the legal document we sign at the same time with two witnesses and the shaikh, which has all the details, such as our names, address, and family information. Then there is also the mahar [dowry]."

The Bahraini Arab dowry amount is determined by the man's level of wealth and not his family's, according to Wafaa. "If he just graduated from the university and has no money, he will take from his father. You can do this. I can do anything I want with the money that he gives to me. I gave it back to him telling him that we were now one, and if ever I needed it I would ask for it back. My mother was very surprised that I gave it back."

Nofa Ghanim al Sulaiti said that in the Arab world, marrying is not just exchanging two rings and hallelujah; you're now married. She says couples are expected to have a big wedding; it's all about the family. "Parents more and more are dictating how much money (mahar) the groom is expected to give to his bride. Being an Arab Bedouin girl means your family is a very old family, which requires a higher amount be paid to marry into that family. They will ask if the girl is Bedouin, Arab, or Arab Bedouin. Our religion is against that actually," she added. "The Prophet said that the less money you pay, the better your marriage will be. But our culture overrides the religion."

"Some women will buy whatever they want with the mahar, especially gold jewelry. Women like the 22-carat yellow gold because, in our culture, gold is very nice," explained Wafaa. "And whenever you are broke, you can sell the gold. So whenever girls in Bahrain have money, they buy gold. Bahraini men don't wear gold. We believe that gold is for ladies and for show, and a man doesn't need either. We had the date and our names engraved on our rings – mine a gold ring and my husband's silver – which is a new tradition. My husband wore his wedding ring the first day and then put it away. This is a common practice, at least with Sunni men."

Culture, ancestry, and religious beliefs have shaped wedding rituals for centuries. Arab historians believe that the primitive Bahraini Arabs came together in the matrimonial bond more for protection and survival than for meaningful relationships. Coinciding with that belief is the theory that the first marriages may have actually been group weddings rather than individual nuptials.

A half century ago Bahraini family life was highly influenced by the traditions of tribal Bedouin society and Islamic ideals and beliefs. Four "serving ladies" [comparable to American bridesmaids] normally carried the bride on a carpet to her husband who would be waiting in a decorated room of red cloth, mirrors, and glass decorative orbs.

Sixty-seven-year-old Fatima Al Janahi described to Asma Salman, a reporter for Bahrain's *Gulfweekly Magazine*, her 1951 wedding, which was typical for the time. Her entire village of about one hundred people was invited to the wedding, which lasted for three days. "On my henna night [the second night], I wore the traditional green handmade, embroidered jalabiya [wedding dress] with the conventional gold jewelry that brides normally wore."

Mrs. Al Janahi wore the Gub Gub [elaborate gold headpiece], the intricate chainmail necklace made of gold coins, and chunky gold bracelets attached to rings on her fingers. A female band performed music on a tara, a traditional hand-held drum, while the girls and women danced in the courtyard. The men were segregated in another area outside of the house. The traditional wedding feast consisted of ghoozi [stuffed whole goat on a bed of rice] accompanied by other local delicacies.

Today, the occasion is a definite blend of local and Western culture – something almost straight out of an American bride's magazine – but modernized.

The twenty-first century Bahraini Muslim bride typically hires a wedding planner, has her wedding at a hotel, wears a white wedding dress, has elaborate flower arrangements, wedding cake, photographer, Western band or DJ, and routinely departs for her honeymoon two days after the reception.

With the high cost of living in Bahrain, mass weddings are becoming more popular as a way to lower the financial burden for those who cannot afford a full-fledged event. There are funds and sponsors, such as banks, corporate bodies, and philanthropists that pay for the wedding expenses, including the food and reception. The Ministry of Education also supports these marriages en masse as they "help strengthen the social aspects of the region." Neighborhood villages come together to wish the grooms well and meet their friends and relatives. An article from the *Bahrain Tribune* [July 3, 2007] written by Alexander M. Arrackal followed six men as they entered marital life. "After the mosque prayers, the grooms retire to their homes, where the bride waits. The brides are not allowed to be in these places, as it is our custom. The grooms, when they join their families for the private celebrations in their homes, are joined by their brides. The dress and the bridal makeup and other adornments are so private that the families do not prefer their daughter being seen by the public."

Divorce and Domestic Violence

With men and women encouraged to marry young – the ideal age for Bahraini girls is eighteen – Americans wonder how marriages can succeed, and whether divorce is recognized in Muslim countries. Both men and women have the right to divorce in the Kingdom of Bahrain; however, women must show cause or else have their husband's permission to divorce.

According to a Bahraini study conducted by the Batelco Centre for Family Violence Victims with published results in the *Gulf Daily News* [June 23, 2007], divorce among Bahrainis [seventy-nine percent of those surveyed] mainly occurs in the first two years of marriage. The most common reason cited for divorce was the inability of the couple to adjust to each other. The majority of women [fifty-two percent] who divorced had not even obtained their high school diploma; forty-seven percent of males had only a high school diploma. In most cases [eighty-one percent], divorced women were granted custody of the children. They were predominantly housewives, while their husbands, although employed, were in unskilled jobs. The study revealed that more than ninety-three percent of women and ninety-five percent of men who filed for divorce were between the ages of twenty-one and thirty. The study also indicated that forty-five percent of women experienced violence during their brief marriages.

Rape, incest, and violence have always existed in the Islamic world. According to Ms. Nada Yateem, a board member of the Aisha Yateem Family Counseling Centre, Arab society has traditionally treated domestic abuse as a private matter, and victims are not provided legal protection. "By bringing this matter [domestic violence] into the open, we want to show that there is a way forward." Bahrain is the only Gulf country that openly offers advocacy and aid to domestic abuse victims.

Dr. Banna Bu Zaboon, president of the Batelco Centre for Family Violence, explained that the study was conducted to determine which factors were associated with divorce, so they can provide the right help and advice to couples and individuals. Dr. Zaboon, who was not surprised by the findings, disclosed that the study also revealed that women don't always get the support they need from those closest to them, as evidenced by 59.7 percent who said that their family was against divorce.

With looming statistics such as these, it was unsettling to read an article in the *Bahrain Tribune* on October 24, 2007, concerning the introduction of Ministerial Order 45 for 2007 by the Minister of Justice and Islamic Affairs determining the age of marriage. The ministerial order set the marriage age for women at fifteen years and for men at eighteen years. The Order has drawn widespread criticism in the Kingdom by religious scholars, Shura Council members, and political activists. Dr. Fakhriya Dairi, president of the Bahrain Centre for Child Protection, was quoted in the *Bahrain Tribune*: "The children are in the learning stage and by marrying them early, their childhood is lost. They cannot complete their studies at fifteen and cannot work after marriage. Early marriage of a girl confines her to household activities and deprives her from education."

Despite these statistics, there are still plenty of Arab Muslims who retain strong convictions toward early marriages. It seems particularly incongruous, since the Arab culture forbids a friendship between the sexes. How can a couple make a marriage work if they have never been allowed to talk or interact on any level with the opposite sex?

One Bahraini in favor of early marriage is Maryam al Sheroogi, the mother of two daughters. "My mother was fifteen when she married. I encourage young girls to marry young because it will prevent a lot of bad things happening to them; it is safer for them," she told me. "I want my daughter to marry when she is fifteen. I want her to be happy in her life when she is young. I don't want her to be twenty-five and getting married. I also want her to have a baby then. I know a lot of people twenty-nine who act like they are twelve, and I know so many more people who are twelve but act like twenty-two. It depends on how you raise your child."

Her friend, Lee Ann Fleetwood, pointed out that American couples choose their mates. "Whether you are happy or not after that, at least the choice was yours. Here, your family brings somebody home and says, 'Okay, this is who you are going to marry.'"

"Actually, it's more about the marriage philosophy before and after marriage," Maryam countered. "For me, the main reason to marry is to have children, but it's also to build a house and career."

Four Wives and Marriageable Cousins

In the Islamic religion, men are permitted to marry up to four women, but with conditions. First, your original wife must agree; secondly, she has been unable to bear sons to continue the family name; and third, she has a cognitive disorder or mental disability that inhibits normal functioning and thought. Everyone I spoke with agreed there must be a good reason [such as those noted] for a man to take an additional wife.

Men think twice before marrying twice, however, as it's difficult having two wives. Most men will tell you that one is challenging enough! But if you do take a second wife, what you give to one, you must give equally. It becomes very expensive.

"If you have a house for one, you have to have a house for the other. If she drives a Honda Civic, the other one gets a Honda Civic; there must be equality in everything: financially, emotionally, and sexually," Nader

Shaheen said as he runs through a mental checklist. "People who tend to have more than one wife either do it because they are very poor or very rich. However, having more than one wife has much more to do with culture, because with high mortality rates, you needed to have more children. If you look at the population pyramid in the developing nations, it is high in mortality with few people in the sixty-five to ninety age range. Few children from that generation survived—which is typical for developing nations. Large families were necessary because so many children died."

Fatima and Rugayah shared the views of the younger generation. Although both girls admitted they would not want to share their husbands with other women, they also qualified their statements with ... "unless there's a good reason."

One scenario they presented was the husband and wife who no longer loved each other, yet the wife did not want a divorce because of the children, so the husband took a second wife.

A second possibility was the husband who was seeing another woman and that woman became pregnant. What would be the best solution for the illegitimate child? Fatima explained that, in the Arab culture, an illegitimate [illegal] child is branded for life and has no rights. So this situation would be a good reason to take a second wife—for the sake of the child. "Take responsibility for what you have done," she said.

Maryam al Sheroogi shared a sad story about a newly divorced friend of hers who was very much in love with her husband, and he with her. They had six daughters together, but using Maryam's words, "The culture pushed him to take another wife so he would have a son."

"And what's so interesting is that the male sperm determines the baby's gender, yet the Arab culture blames the woman when she only has girls," pointed out the incredulous Lee Ann Fleetwood.

Islam allows marriage between cousins. Although at first this concept may sound disturbing, there is definitely some logic behind it. "When Islam first began, Arabs were Bedouin tribes wandering in the deserts," Fleetwood explained. "They had power in numbers. The larger the tribe, the more power they possessed. Women were viewed as inheritable property, so obviously tribes did not want to lose them to another tribe when it came time for her to marry. Afterall, they were "breeders" who would enlarge the tribe's numbers. If she married outside of the tribe, not only would the tribe lose her wealth, but it would also make another tribe richer. The best solution then was to marry her to a tribe member. With tribes consisting mainly of large extended families, it was easier to marry cousins, and they were also the closest in line under the Quran's stated inheritance laws. So women retained their status and breeding abilities within the tribe, and the wealth remained intact."

Separate Sexes

"As a mother of four boys and four girls who I have always viewed as equal in talent, intelligence, and opportunity, " Wisconsinite Agnes Kennard asked, "How are the sexes viewed in Bahrain? Are they 'equal' in 'their place' only, and is that 'place' restricted by religion and/or society?"

Maryam al Sheroogi responded, "Our culture says we cannot have a friendship between boys and girls. We cannot change our culture because Islam is inside of it. I don't want to change our culture. In this culture, we believe that any man who will be with any woman will bother her. The Hadith says a woman can't be with a man alone. Because of this, a lot of Bahrainis and Arabs don't let their kids stay at anybody's house."

"You assume that friendship means sex," Fleetwood countered. "Everything in this society is based on prevention of sex. All of your rules are based on suspicion and not trusting individuals to make their own choices and be able to control their own behavior."

"As a social worker, I saw so many abused women," replied Maryam. "That's why we protect our daughters by not allowing them to see men in any house; even in my brother's house. He knows that my daughter cannot be alone with him. I don't know what might happen. That's why she is always between my eyes. Nowadays in the Arab society, we don't trust men. We say prevention is better than the treatment. We try to teach our girls not to let any man touch them. We educate them to be careful. Then, when they are older, they understand that."

At this point in the conversation between these women, I wanted to be sure I understood what I was hearing. Maryam expressed fear that a man or boy looking at her four-year-old daughter will have "bad ideas," as she put it. The majority of American men do not think of four-year-olds as sexual beings. And if they do, and sexually molest a child, such convicted pedophiles go to jail for a very long time. There appeared to be no concept of this behavior being wrong regardless of the age of the girl in this Arab country's culture. Newspaper accounts frequently tell of rapists being freed for lack of witnesses or, worse yet, the victim's father "forgives" the rapist.

"We don't trust any men. That's why even in the house she should be between my eyes always, and I should protect her," repeated Maryam.

I asked what would happen to an Arab man who was molesting an eight- or twelve-year-old girl in Bahrain.

"By law he would go to jail, but the culture will judge the girl, even if she is a child," explained Maryam. "That's why most families hide it if it has happened, because it is a shame on the girl, not the boy or male."

Lee Ann concurred with Maryam's assessment, adding, "Anyone living here in the Arab world is aware of the stigma associated with victims of rape or any sexual misconduct, regardless of how it occurred. Women are not seen as victims, but rather as co-conspirators in the crime, and thus are less likely to report such an incident if it happens."

"You see, for women, there are conditions for everything," Maryam continued. "We cannot have a friendship with boys. We cannot swim with boys in public. We cannot ride a bike in public. We cannot play sports in public. I used to play basketball and squash inside my house; I was a squash player in college. The problem is not only mine. In the culture here, men feel they have all the control. They are extreme in the Arab culture;

they try to control women."

Zaman M. Munawar provided his thoughts via newspaper editorial: "Islam allows for healthy games without discrimination, but only and when these are within the limit of ethics. To avoid the dispersal of a sexually encouraging environment, it [Islam] even prohibits thinking, watching, reading, and listening to all the stuff that ultimately leads to complete involvement. Gone is the time when children were innocent. I, as a husband, brother, and father who loves his family, can never, ever allow others to come see and enjoy the bodies and movement of my own family members. If ladies of my family want [to play sports], I have to provide them with all facilities indoors, where they can play and enjoy easily."

An Arab man, who wished to remain anonymous and admitted being conservative, cited an example of what he felt was very wrong in Manama [Bahrain's capital city]. A high-rise building was proposed in an area where a girls' school was located. This Muslim was concerned about privacy issues for the female students since people in the high-rise would be able to look out and upon the girls' school property. His opinion was that Bahrain is a conservative society that values privacy, and that should not change. Hence, the high-rise building should not be constructed.

"Some of my aunties won't shake my hand or touch it," disclosed Nader Shaheen, referring to some Muslim women and their cultural choices. "Some women in the Souq markets and the grocery checkout will drop the coins into my hand. They won't place the money in my hand; they drop it. They want no contact with men. This is culture, and they have made a cultural choice. All religions evolved this way."

› Religion is religion,
custom is custom,
tradition is tradition,
but no two people
think in exactly
the same way. ‹

Phoebe Boswell

Author of

Bahrainona: Drawing from Life

CHAPTER 4

Hijab and Traditional Dress

Many Americans are bewildered by the unfamiliar sight of Arab Muslim women garbed in black. Frown lines form and heads shake in disbelief at the sight of a woman in niqab (face covering). It seems strange. Why on earth would a woman dress like that?

It's a well-known assumption in the Arab world that Arab men by nature are jealous creatures. According to Nofa al Sulaiti, many of the reasons a woman would wear hijab are due to the way Arab *MEN* were raised. "Men were raised to believe that women should cover up. The new generation is trying to change that, and men are not as jealous as they were before. The men today are more open-minded," she reported. "The generation of men now lets the whole family travel, go into restaurants and public places and sit and eat together. In the early days, no man was allowed to look at another's wife. She should cover up, even her face. Why? *He* was raised that way. When he was a young boy, he could not look at girls, even his cousins, because he might marry one of them some day. But as a young teen, he looked at girls and thought they were pretty or nice. So when he grew up and married, he didn't want other men looking at his wife and thinking of her as he used to think when he looked at girls."

AMERICAN Generalization #3

Women who veil themselves are forced to and are oppressed. And those that completely veil themselves are scary looking.

Is it that they are in black that Americans think they look scary? Something reminiscent of a funeral? Is it the fear of the unknown or merely curiosity about what is beneath the abaya? Or is it that we can't see their faces or hair? Are they covering themselves because of a self-esteem problem? Do their husbands and/or family force them to dress like this?

Many questions and scenarios tug at American minds. It is a simple case of genuine ignorance. We simply do not know.

Of course, if one reverts back into history, just about all religions at some point had women wearing some type of veil. Mary, the mother of Jesus, is usually depicted in Christian art with her head covered. By the Middle Ages, Jewish women largely conformed to the custom of hair covering. Until the 1960s, it was obligatory for Catholic girls and women to cover their heads in church. Catholic nuns for centuries wore floor length black habits and had their hair covered. I grew up Catholic and attended Catholic schools, so I didn't find nuns scary looking. However, nuns in full black habits were indeed scary looking to many of my non-Catholic friends.

Traditional Hindu women still cover their heads and at least partly obscure their faces around unrelated adult males. A large number of African women wear headscarves, as do many Russian women.

"Some women are forced to wear hijab," admitted Wafaa Ashoor. "Not the majority of them, but some are still forced. Some fathers force their daughters to wear niqab even today. For hijab, I think the father should insist because this is for his daughter's benefit. Now or later she will know it was the right thing to do and thank him. But to cover her entire face? No, this is not general practice. But there are still some men who force it."

Rania Noor contended that hijab is a statement of a Muslim woman's identity, and that "anyone who sees her will know she is a Muslim and has a good moral character. Many Muslim women who cover are filled with dignity and self-esteem; they are pleased to be identified as Muslim women. As a chaste, modest, pure woman, she does not want her sexuality to enter into interactions with men in even the smallest degree. A woman who covers herself is concealing her sexuality, but allowing her femininity to be revealed. Hijab is not merely a covering, but more importantly, it is behavior, manners, speech, and appearance in public. Dress is only one facet of the total being."

"The hijab is a very difficult issue for us," said Maryam al Sheroogi. "For many, they believe if they removed their hijab, hell would come to them."

"But many girls now know why they have to wear it," added Wafaa Ashoor. "We must explain to our daughters not only why they should wear hijab, but also tell them they have to put it on. It's not that hard. When I was growing up, people knew it was in the Book about wearing hijab, but they didn't know *why* women were supposed to wear it. But everybody knows now what is in the Book. It's in our nature to want to do what's in the Book, so we are returning to the Book."

I asked Wafaa for her perspective as a mother on what she would do if she had a daughter who wore hijab when she left the house and then later she saw her daughter at the mall without it. I also asked what her husband would do given the same scenario.

"I would grab her and take her to a coffee shop and ask her to explain to me why she wasn't wearing it. I would let her know that I want her to wear it and ask her why she thinks it is not easy for her to do so. If she won't wear it, what can I do? I can't force her to wear it.

"If it was my husband who saw her, he would tell her to go directly home and that he would see her later. My husband would not discuss it in the coffee shop. Once home, he would come to me, as he would never speak to her without me being present. All of our discussions would have to be among the three of us. This is my husband's way. If my daughter has a different opinion, she will speak up and tell her father that when he and I come to talk to her."

Twenty-one-year-old Nofa al Sulaiti does not wear hijab, although her mother does. I asked her if that presented any tensions between mother and daughter. "Every single day before I go to the university, my mother says something. It's a very difficult decision to make. The hijab is a commitment for me. So if I wear it, I will cover all of my hair and all of my body. Some of the girls in Bahrain – especially the Bedouin girls – do this not for the religion and not for God, but for their reputation and their family. Example; I'm doing this for my family; I'm doing this for my mother; I'm doing this because of my family name; the women in my family always wore hijab. This is what is happening right now.

"If I wear hijab, I will wear it the right way like I'm supposed to wear it, not like the girls do with their hair showing. If I decide to wear hijab, I will wear it for God and not for people. But I have to think carefully about it, because if I put it on and I'm not confident enough, I might take it off. And this is not good. People might have a bad impression of me and say 'Yeah, she used to wear it and now she doesn't. What's going on?' I won't wear it because my mother told me to or because I have to for my family name."

Naseem, Nofa's mother, said she realizes that she cannot force her daughter to cover. "She'll go out and take it off, and I don't want that. But I think that here in Bahrain wearing hijab is more tradition than religion."

What if you were married and your husband forced you to wear it, I asked Nofa. "Actually, this is not the point," she answered. "Before we marry, we would discuss it. If I like this person and want him as my husband, and he told me after we were married, would you please do this as an honor for my family and for me, of course, I would. But if after we were married he decided he wanted me to wear it, then that's a big problem. Then it's like he is forcing me, and I won't like that. I'm actually planning to wear hijab whenever I do get married."

"You know, some women who wear hijab look sexier than the ladies who don't," Salah Al Shuroogi told me. "There are some beautiful eyes. And yes, some people think they do look scary. We are no longer a small village; Muslim people travel the world just as American and Europeans do. I would ask the American people to accept and live with hijabbed women and not to harass women they might see like this."

Nofa also weighs in on the makeup issue as she herself wears makeup and has beautifully highlighted eyes: "Girls and women can wear makeup, but on limited areas. For example, black eyeliner is halal, which means okay. This is a cultural thing, not a religious thing. Prophet Muhammad said this was the culture before Islam, but that women should not wear too much of it. It was the Bedouin culture to wear eyeliner. They also had an herb that women wore, called dorim, that made your lips brownish orange. In the Arab world specifically, because of the way we dress [wearing an abaya] and covering our hair, what's the part of your body that is seen the most? The face. So girls want to highlight that as best they can to show off. Yeah, it's a contradiction within our culture because when we put on the hijab the main idea of wearing it is to prevent men from staring at us. So when we wear makeup ... well then, the point is — why are you wearing hijab in the first place?"

Apparently Arab Muslims know Americans well, as this generalization popped up on their list, too, about Americans.

ARAB Generalization #4

Americans believe that Muslim women who cover themselves are backward.

To most Americans, it seems as though women in hijab (headscarf) or niqab (full face veil) and those wearing an abaya (black robe) appear to be more subservient when covered.

"I am a Muslim Bahraini wife and mother," Eman wrote, "And I dress the way I feel I want to dress. Allah will judge me for my behavior, my good deeds, and my clean heart and mind."

Yet another Muslim woman, who wished to remain anonymous, said, "According to Islam, women should be covered from head to toe if they are in front of any men. This helps protect a woman's body parts from men. It is a shield that protects a woman from evil thinking or the stares of men. Allah Almighty has ordered women to cover themselves; so who has the right to say what is wrong and what is right? Furthermore, covering oneself doesn't mean that we Muslims are not modern or 'backward' as many Europeans and Americans think."

In addition, the Americans I interviewed felt the hijabbed Arab Muslim women had a limited education (the mandatory grades until high school graduation) and then were pressured into marrying and immediately starting a family.

The Bahraini Muslim women – at least those in their twenties – that I interviewed are well educated with jobs and career aspirations. Many Americans think the majority of these women are uneducated and at home caring for their family and husband, and that's the extent of their life.

"I really think Americans have the misconception that Arab women are not that highly educated, and for some reason seeing them in scarves and an abaya contributes to that misperception," said Joan Corey, an American.

"That's an interesting concept about women," remarked Lee Ann Fleetwood after reading the two generalizations. "Americans may think that Arab women are oppressed because they wear hijab. But then Arab Muslims feel that American women are repressed because they have to use their bodies in every aspect of their lives. It depends on which side of the coin you are looking at. Personally, if I had to choose between walking around half naked and walking around covered, I'd prefer the covered. I don't believe in the extreme form of covering, but at the same time, I find it disgusting that every advertisement in America from socks to cars has a half naked woman in it. Why aren't there men in underwear trying to get us to buy a car?"

"And that is what we Arabs say about the Americans," echoed Maryam al Sheroogi. "Why do you consider your women cheap?"

To wear or not wear hijab is a hotly contested issue in this Arab country with no apparent right or wrong reason. There are extreme opinions waged against the more liberal viewpoints, and degrees of everything in between. Again, it comes down to religion versus culture.

What follows are theological opinions, broad generalizations, Muslim women making impassioned pleas to their "sisters" to wear hijab and abayas, and even some men weighing in on the topic. It is becoming more obvious that the Islamic dress code is not rigidly defined; rather the emphasis seems to be on women dressing modestly – and how can that be a black and white decision?

Culture or Religion?

"I believe the Quran says to cover that which you consider private," ventured Nader Shaheen. "And in some references it's translated as covering your breasts as well. At the time it wasn't uncommon for women to be topless, which nowadays – even in the West – is too much. But it's culture and not religion. Cover your head, cover your face, cover your hands – completely black out – no one could point that out in the Quran. No one can show you where it says completely cover yourself from head to toe in black, because it doesn't exist. Therefore, this is culture. It is not about religion. It is a sprout seed that has gone to seed, and something that someone has run with and just kept going. It is not against our secular law to go out with your hair showing, wearing jeans, and a T-shirt. You cannot be arrested for that in Bahrain.

"Christianity and other religions are practiced in a hundred different ways around the world. Where the culture will affect it, it manifests itself in wearing the veil. To my understanding, it is not a pre-requisite for being a good Muslim. There are basic and decent things about culture that are vastly more important than whether or not you expose your hair. Do you donate to charity? Do you try to do good works for the poor? Don't steal, don't lie – the basic things – those are much more important."

Lee Ann Fleetwood offered some background history: "Muslims back in the day were being harassed by those intent on keeping Islam from spreading. Muslim women were especially harassed as they were seen as the weaker gender. Arabia in those days was barbaric and very open concerning sexuality. It is well known that women walked around with their chests exposed and nobody thought too much about it. In general, the dress of the time was fairly casual.

"Women wore a cloth that draped over their heads because of the arid, hot conditions of the region. It had nothing to do with religion. It was not held securely around the body or used to cover the hair; most often it hung loosely down and provided protection from the elements.

"Slave women in those days were considered fair game to anyone. Non-Muslims used that as an excuse to avoid blame when they harassed Muslim women, claiming that they couldn't tell Muslim from non-Muslim or slaves. Muslim women appealed to the Prophet to find a solution fearing the harassment would intensify. He prayed to Allah for guidance and the message was that Allah wants the Muslim women to cover their chests and dress modestly so that aggressors to Islam will have no further excuse for causing harm.

"Allah tells them to use the same cloth that they've always used and just bring it over their chests in a more modest fashion. The ultimate aim was to distinguish Muslim women from non-Muslim and slaves. You have to wonder that nowadays its hijabbed and veiled women that are most likely to be harassed because of the distinction, so maybe the opposite holds true now.

"There are Muslims now and from the past who sincerely believe that Allah never ordered hijab to be worn, and so it is a choice for them to wear it or not, and they believe they will not be punished for it. It should not be considered a deficiency in their religion just because others believe it is ordered.

"Allah orders modest dress, modest behavior, and justice to be done between us. We know that covering ourselves from head to toe in black has no magical effect on men who are intent to cause harm. What we need to do is raise our Muslim sons to have "hijab" of the heart and mind concerning women, and then the two genders could coexist in a true Islamic society in which women are free to expose their hair without the burden of being seen as deficient or fair game, but still queens and due equal respect as hijabis.

"The Quran does not tell women to wear the hijab and to cover their heads and hair. It's just not there. Hijab for women did not even become a widespread practice until more than two hundred years after the Prophet's death. And it was a cultural practice new converts to Islam used to show the difference between rich women and poor. If it was a direct order from God, then for sure all Muslim women alive at the time of the Prophet would have practiced it without a second thought, and so would Muslim women forever after that. But it wasn't and it isn't," concluded Fleetwood.

Fatima Ali and Rugayah Sharif discussed the philosophy in their respective Shia families that they experienced as to wearing hijab when they were younger.

"My mother said, 'I will not tell you to wear the scarf'," began Rugayah. "'I want you to come and tell me that you want to wear it.' If I want to wear the scarf, then I have to wear it and never remove it. It was a hard decision at first. But once a girl wears it, she becomes attached to it and doesn't think of removing it. People will ask me--aren't you hot wearing it? Well the thing is, I sometimes forget I'm wearing it; it has become part of my body."

"I feel weird sometimes if I don't wear it," Fatima admitted. "You either always wear it or never wear it. It's an attitude, a way of living. The scarf is not just a piece of clothing that you occasionally wear. Sometimes I'll see a woman not wearing one and she respects herself; I can tell by her pose and the way she carries herself. Then there's a girl wearing a scarf because she was told to, and my God, it is obvious that there is no respect!

"A lot depends on the upbringing as to whether you wear it or not. Some parents are very open and others are very strict. For some it's more of a negotiation; don't go out without one because of a, b, and/or c, and they try to convince their child like that. I will not wear something that I am not convinced of. If my mother tells me that I have to wear the scarf, I won't necessarily because my mother is not here with me this very minute. I can take it off whenever I want. And that's what happens, I think, for most girls if they've been forced into wearing it. You cannot force things upon people, but if I'm convinced about the reasons for wearing it, then why not? It all depends on your upbringing."

"I know families who are very restrictive with their daughters," Rugayah added. "At home they are told to wear the scarf, not use the mobile; they can't go outside with their friends, but as soon as they go off to the university, they rebel. Off comes the scarf."

"I believe that our religion says women must cover their hair," she continued. "I want to protect myself. Here in Bahrain they say that the hair is the cause of evil thoughts. So when you see a girl with long hair, you know guys are looking at her. We may be innocent, but we are not naïve."

When I asked what's so bad about looking at a girl's hair, Rugayah's answer was short and succinct: "A guy's blood runs in only two directions. Wearing a scarf is a cultural thing. If I see a woman not wearing one, and she is respecting herself by the way she acts or dresses, I'm not going to judge her or say she's a bad Muslim because she's not wearing a scarf."

In Bahrain if a Shia girl is going to wear hijab, it usually happens around age nine, but Fatima and Rugayah were eleven and Naeema, Fatima's younger sister, was twelve years old. They explained that their parents did not want to push them.

Although these three young adults do not customarily wear an abaya, they sometimes will. Fatima usually wears it when she goes to the Souq, while Rugayah sheepishly admitted she wears one when she's running late for work.

"There are beautiful abayas that are very fashionable with embroidery and in different colors. Sometimes you can feel more fashionable wearing one rather than the same old thing," said Fatima.

"Women who wear an abaya can remove it whenever they want, but they're used to it. They feel that if they are not wearing one, it's like they are walking around naked. In some families, girls are not allowed to remove their abayas. And they really aren't that hot in the summer; they have some material that is really quite light like the material in a pair of shorts."

"I am a Bahraini Muslim girl," wrote Maha, "And have been wearing a hijab and abaya since I was a teenager. I swear I really feel safe and valuable each time I wear them. I have beautiful hair with a healthy body that strictly should not be seen by strangers, because it is a gift from Allah and a part of respecting His holy instructions. You know that a girl is like a diamond that must always be covered with a veil of silk to protect it. It is important to mention here that not only Islam urges women to cover their hair; the Bible also does. To sum up, I feel like a princess under the umbrella of Islam and its teachings to wear hijab."

Najiya, who chose not to disclose her last name, said that Islam is more cultural than religious. "When it comes to practicing faith, we have to follow the rules laid down in the Quran and Hadith. It is from the very authentic Hadith that we get our dress code. We wear the abaya as a shapeless black garment so that it hides the very shapely us. We don't want any non-mahrem [non-related] men seeing how we look."

Another Muslim woman, Maria, noted that all religions, including Christianity and Judaism, value the modest and chaste nature of the woman. "Muslim women everywhere are proud to wear their beautiful and modest Islamic dress, both as a way of identifying themselves as Muslims and as a shield against envious or lustful glances."

"The hijab has an indispensable function in the life of a Muslim woman," offered Ameena Ali. "That is protection and preservation of her honor and chastity. This means that a woman who wears the hijab does not do this to declare her religion or distinguish herself. Rather, she wears it out of obedience to her Lord."

An anonymous male offered his opinion to the hijab debate: "Being a man, I must say that we actually have more respect for women who do cover up properly rather than those who do not. Men generally try to flirt with those who expose themselves. We don't want the risk of being embarrassed by flirting with a woman who is covering herself; she might actually be a respectful, true Muslim who is probably married."

Rasool Hassan, married with three children, has never suggested to his wife that she wear or not wear hijab or an abaya. "Because she grew up in a family where they wanted her to wear one, it became part of her life. Sometimes she only wears a scarf to cover her hair. It's her decision. But to be very honest with you, as a Muslim man, I prefer that she wear both an abaya and a scarf. I think it's nice to see that. Islam does not have a problem with women not wearing an abaya, as long as she is wearing good clothing – nothing tight or short – that respects her and others. I have no problem with that. I have seen midriff tops and low-cut tops on eighteen- and twenty-year-old girls out at the mall – really unbelievable – and because of the way they dress, this could lead to problems. I'm not saying they should be wearing an abaya or scarf to protect themselves from men staring. Whether one wears an abaya or a tent, you'll not stop a man from staring."

Jemma, an Arab Muslim, said, "Muslim women see their mode of dress as a form of freedom from the unrelenting form of obsession and objectification of the female body. It stresses the profound worth of the inner person and reduces the fixation of physical/material factors."

I have seen (more than once) the allure that a prim and proper woman in niqab can produce with heavily made up eyes as she casts a single, darting glance with seductively flirting eyes. Conversely, a cold glance can put a man in his rightful place with the same eyes of a woman in casual Western attire.

An anonymous woman offered an extreme view that the practice of unveiling is *harmful* to Bahraini society. "Women are taught from early childhood that their worth is proportional to their attractiveness. We feel compelled to pursue abstract notions of beauty; half realizing that such a pursuit is futile. Mothers who compel their daughters to take off the hijab, saying that they won't find husbands wearing it, are not educating their daughters to obey Allah and his messenger. If a woman will not obey Allah and his messenger, how can she be expected to obey her husband? The honor of a father is his daughter. The honor of a brother is his sister. The honor of a husband is his wife, and the honor of a son is his mother. Remember that when you leave the hijab and show the shape of your body (wearing jeans and T-shirts or even a tight fitting abaya) or, worse still, your hair and skin, then you are in fact dishonoring and insulting your fathers, brothers, sons, and husbands."

Lee Ann Fleetwood took issue with this opinion, countering, "Honor should not be a burden on another person."

Annie Coyle, an Irish woman teaching Bahraini Arab adults conversational English, noted that in the past few years she has seen more women wearing hijab at the universities than previously. She wonders if it is from society's cultural pressure rather than religious belief. "I don't think anybody would ask anyone to change his or her culture. I think maybe the point is whether we have the right to judge another's culture. You have the choice to wear whatever you want, and respect what other people are wearing, without thinking that your way is the only right way. You should respect the culture that you live in."

"In Bahrain most women involved in public life and who have been well educated dress as they wish," contended Saara, who does not wear hijab. "Some wear abayas, some wear long and loose Western clothing, some wear tighter Western clothing, some cover their hair, and some don't. And yet, all dress within an acceptable range of "modesty." No one seems particularly concerned about dress, and I'm sure it is a non-issue for many.

"It seems that when a woman has achieved something worthwhile, it is almost an unspoken rule not to discuss her appearance. This does not mean that one's dress is entirely unimportant. It is just that it should never be the absolute emphasis of one's identity as a person. The inside is just as important as the outside."

"People in this country want you to wear hijab not for God, but for society and for them," contended Lee Ann Fleetwood. "I told my daughters that I didn't believe in it and I don't wear it, but I will not make the choice for them. My oldest daughter removed her headscarf for a month or so awhile back and got a lot of grief for that. She actually lost a friend over it, which really angered me. This friend told my daughter that 'if you were my friend, you would wear your hijab.' She should have said if you are a Muslim and you believe in God, you would wear it, not that if you want to be my friend you'll wear it.

"God says over and over in the Quran that He is the Most Fair, the Most Merciful, the Most Loving – every good word you can think about God – and He also says He does not distinguish between the genders; He makes them equal. He says that we are accountable for our own behavior, and that each of us should behave ourselves, lower our gaze, don't look at forbidden things, and don't partake in forbidden acts. We should all behave modestly at all times. So given that He spent the whole entire Book telling us how to behave ourselves, why then would He say, 'but because men are weak and always want sex and can't control themselves, in this case women should cover up their entire bodies and not let men see them?'

"Well, men shouldn't be looking at women's bodies. God already explained that. They should be behaving themselves, and God said that, too. If women's hair is sexy to men, then men's hair is sexy to women. So why don't men have to cover up from us? And also, don't forget that God is going to hold each individual accountable. You are not accountable for every man in this room if he looks at you. It is their sin if they look at you, not yours. As long as you dress modestly and behave modestly, it is not your sin if a man looks at you and thinks immodestly."

"This is what you see," countered Maryam al Sheroogi. "We see something else. In the old days of our culture, if a man saw a woman dressed provocatively, he would give her a poem about her body and her beauty. That poem brought shame to the girl's family because everybody knew the poem was about her. The Arabic poem is very bad."

"In Irish society, because it is normal to be uncovered, most men don't look at us," interjected Annie Coyle. "In general, you could walk around all day looking provocative and men don't notice because it is natural. So we are not a temptation to every man. I wasn't brought up to think of myself as tempting or having that much power. Do you think as an Arab woman that you are that powerful in terms of your beauty and sexuality that you have to cover it up?"

"No," replied Maryam. "We feel that only because God says we should wear hijab and cover that we cover. That is what we believe. Even we don't think that we are that beautiful and are covering because of this. We cover because the Quran says we should cover."

"Why do you see men as being sexually tempted by women, but women not sexually tempted by men, Maryam?" Lee Ann asked. "I find men damn hot;

why should I cover myself from them? Of course, women find men sexy, but are we asexual that we don't have sexual feelings? You are saying that women should cover themselves up so men don't find them sexual, but women find men sexual as well. So why shouldn't men cover up?"

Should Men Cover Up?

"The basic requirements of the Muslim woman's dress apply to the Muslim man's clothing with the difference being mainly in degree," explained Rania Noor. "Modesty requires that the area between the navel and the knee be covered in front of all people except the wife. The clothing of men should not be like the dress of women, nor should it be tight or provocative.

"A man should dress to show his identity as a Muslim. Men's clothing requirements are not meant to be a restriction, but rather a way in which society will function in a proper, Islamic manner."

It is not compulsory in Bahrain for Muslim men to wear the traditional thoub (robe) or the head scarf (kathra). Does that make it a double standard? Maybe; maybe not. It is quite common though to see young men in their late teens and early twenties wearing a thoub and baseball cap on the streets and in the shopping malls, or a thoub and nothing on their head. But there are also many more in casual Western attire. And there seems to be no public outcry or heated debate regarding men's dress as exists with women.

I asked both Hameed Alawi and Rasool Hassan if they grew up wearing traditional dress, since neither wore it when I met them. Rasool always wears Western clothing, he told me, but was unable to explain why. "I don't know why I don't wear traditional; I've never asked myself that question. My father always wore traditional dress; I grew up seeing that. He wore Western style clothing to work, but as soon as he got home in the evening, he switched to traditional. As a child, I wore traditional dress, and my family wears it. I guess I just don't feel comfortable wearing it."

I asked if he would have his two sons wear traditional dress as children. "I'm not going to dictate that; if they want to, then yes. Actually, my five-year-old asked me last week to take him to the shop and buy him traditional clothes."

I have met a number of Bahraini Muslim men and often wondered why one day I'd see them in traditional dress and on other days in Western clothing. I put the question to Rasool. "It is nothing really," he explained, "especially in Bahrain. If you compare us with the GCC [Gulf Cooperation Council] countries of the UAE, Qatar, Oman, Kuwait, and Saudi Arabia, there are no problems if we wear or do not wear traditional. In some GCC countries though, if you don't wear the traditional clothing, you won't be treated as nicely as a man who wears the traditional. I have seen that firsthand in Dubai."

Alawi wears both traditional and Western clothing, although he qualified his statement: "I mostly wear Western clothes, except when I have a meeting with someone in the Ministry. I feel that people in the Ministry are more traditional, so I wear traditional dress then. I don't wear traditional clothes at home, mostly jeans and shirts or shorts when it is very hot. During the Eid after Ramadan, I wear traditional clothes."

He also grew up in a family where the men wore traditional dress. His father wears a thoub. "As a young boy, my father wanted me to wear a thoub also, but I didn't find it comfortable then, and so I didn't wear it. In school, of course, we wore uniforms. So I decided at an early age that I did not want to wear it. My father understands that and is okay with my decision. I have four brothers, and they trade off between casual clothing and traditional dress."

Regardless of how one views the issue of clothing for men and women, listening carefully during my interviews and observing others, I definitely saw the 'I am right, you are wrong' attitude. As an American woman, my takeaway on this hotly-debated topic was certainly not to brand those who wear hijab and abaya as backward, but to understand that it is a very personal decision for each Muslim girl and woman. From a Muslim point of view, hijab is not magic. Covering oneself is no guarantee of protection from unwanted stares from men or the whispering tongues of women.

Whether the hijab and abaya were prescribed by God, influenced by thousands of years of tradition and culture, or a combination of both, it's obvious that the way Muslim women dress in the Bahraini Arab world is not going to change any time soon. As culture changes in Bahrain, it will happen very, very slowly, if at all.

» Illiteracy keeps women in the dark about their rights and keeps them docile and controllable. «

Lee Ann Fleetwood

CHAPTER 5

Education, Women's Rights, and Empowerment

Islam instructs women and men to seek knowledge, whether religious or secular, which will benefit them in their lives. Assuming that Arab Muslims recognize the importance and value that Islam has placed on religious knowledge since the earliest days, secular education now is the focus of knowledge.

The Kingdom of Bahrain set up its first boys' school in 1919 with the first girls' school opening nine years later. The first American school in the Gulf – The American Mission School – was established in Bahrain. The Modern Knowledge School is another American school beginning with kindergarten that features an American educational curriculum. Many Arab families (including Saudi Arabs) recognize the value of the American education system and send their children to Bahraini schools with such a curriculum.

Education, particularly college and beyond, has been held in high regard across the Kingdom for decades.

"Sixty years ago it wasn't like that," agreed Fatima Ali and Rugayah Sharif. "According to our mothers, women were not allowed to study, although it had nothing to do with the religion. It was the culture. Instructors asked themselves what is it that children need to know, and that is what students were taught. But that's not our culture now."

From those I spoke with, it appeared that if the parents were college educated, so usually were their children. For example, Fatima's mother has a college degree, and her father has two degrees. One uncle has a professorship. She and her sister both have their bachelor of science degrees, and to them that is the minimum. "A B.S. degree is like a high school diploma for us now," Fatima said, "As we are all aiming for a master's or Ph.D. It used to be that if you had a high school degree, you could get a good job. Not any more; now if you don't have a master's degree, you have a lousy job."

The Ali sisters grew up in a family atmosphere that promoted the value of education. Fatima recalled as a young girl never hearing her relatives say that they hoped to see her in her wedding gown some day. Rather, they said they hoped to see her Ph.D. The education seed was firmly planted in early childhood, and nourished from then on.

Rugayah had the same lofty educational ambitions, while noting that some of her friends do not share her views. As she put it, "They would rather be seen and get married."

Engineer Rasool Hassan believed strongly in preparing his children while young, as part of Bahrain's future generation, to become leaders in society as adults. "As a father, I want my children to reach a level that I could not reach. To prepare them for that, I believe, is to enlist studying and schooling, and then university study. It is very expensive to live in Bahrain, and I cannot secure their futures by buying land or properties for them. Promoting studying and advanced education is something that all parents can do while their children are young."

That concept presents a challenge to many Bahrainis who thirty years ago just wanted to work hard and provide a comfortable life for their families. "I think it was more of a financial reason why thirty to thirty-five years ago most Bahrainis did not go to college. Although grade school and secondary schooling is free in the government schools, the university is not. If a student scores high marks, it's possible to attend college on a scholarship. But if your grades are not tops, then you need to pay to go to the university," he explained.

"Back then you might find two parents with nine or twelve kids. Life was much simpler, and they enjoyed a good quality of life," Hassan continued.

"You would never find people without food because back then everyone lived in villages. We were all one big extended family. For example, if someone came to our house to visit, and my mother did not have enough food on hand, we'd go to our neighbor and take from him. This was the simplest life I have ever experienced."

For those opting for a college education versus marrying right out of high school, the financial implications and Bahrain's high cost of living make the final decision a bit easier.

"If you know you are going on to college, it's best not to have a girlfriend or someone you need to support," Hameed Alawi explained. "With the financial difficulties and what things cost in Bahrain, you are better off to complete your education. Once that is finished, you are in a situation to find a good position with a company or start your own business. It is very difficult to be married and try to support a wife, and maybe even a child, while going to college. For one thing, rental rates for flats are very high."

ARAB Generalization #5

American students are expected to take a part-time job in high school, and move out when they graduate or turn eighteen.

The twenty-somethings who were in college or are recent graduates firmly believed and felt sorry for American students as regard to the above generalization. Based on conversations with Americans, this Arab generalization holds some truth.

Many Americans graduating from high school in the '60s and early '70s moved out of the family home and were on their own at eighteen (myself included). I remember that if I were not going on to college, my next viable option was marriage. Those of us who did go to college either lived on campus or at home with our parents. In the early 1970s in Minnesota and Wisconsin, where I grew up, the middle class, blue-collar family consensus leaned more toward finding a job after high school. A woman wanting a "career" was a less familiar concept.

Today, more young adults in the U.S., whether in college or the work force, choose to live at home with their families. According to a survey conducted in March 2007 by *Glamour* magazine, forty-six percent of women under the age of twenty-five still lived at home with their parents. Furthermore, the survey found that the average age an American woman marries is twenty-five, while seventy-four percent of college-educated women waited until after age twenty-nine.

The Americans I interviewed had no problem understanding why other cultures have the perception, as listed in the above generalization, simply because that's the way it used to be – at least in the Midwest where my group of interviewees hail from – although it is no longer the norm. As Minnesotan Joan Corey noted, "Kids today can't afford to live alone anymore; a lot of them have to come back home after moving out."

In Bahrain, high school students are not expected to take a part-time job. It is a father's responsibility to support his children until they marry. And because of the Arab culture's emphasis on family, women do not live outside the home unless married. Most men do not either. Exceptions, of course, include those who have gone abroad to college.

According to Fatima and Rugayah, if their families are experiencing financial difficulties, and young adults living at home are employed, they help out financially — because they want to and not because they are obligated to. "The salary is the individual's, if he or she wants to contribute toward the family expenses, it is up to the individual," said Rugayah.

"I think this generalization is positive," replied Wafaa Ashoor. "I think it's nice that students work, but not that they leave home. That is not the norm here in Bahrain. Here the father supports the children. My son is twenty-five, and my husband supports him with food and clothing and gives him the car."

In regard to the Bahraini tradition of children remaining at home until marriage, I asked Mrs. Ashoor how a young man learns responsibility for supporting a wife and future family, and understands its importance when he has not had to do so.

"Because he saw his father, he will copy him," she answered. "Even my husband is copying what his father did. When you are raised in that environment, you know. Bahrainis have large extended families. We support our children; we will never leave them alone."

AMERICAN Generalization #4

The Arabs hate Americans, but they sure want an American education.

The generalization as it stands is born of fear and ignorance. The statement needs to be broken down into its two parts and addressed separately, contended Nader Shaheen.

The Arabs hate Americans? "No," said the Bahrainis I talked with. The Arabs may certainly hate American foreign policy, but do not hate the American people. [Foreign policy is addressed elsewhere.]

"No, no," replied Wafaa Ashoor, when asked if Arabs hate Americans. "This is not a true statement. If we are true Muslims, we cannot hate. There is no hate in Islam."

Salah Al Shuroogi also weighed in on the above generalization. "Generally, we live and work with a lot of Americans in the Gulf, and they are very good people. They are like us – they are open – and will not hide anything. We don't hate Americans. The problem lies in the policies of the American politicians."

I found the second part about Arabs wanting an American education to be true among the Bahrainis interviewed. I see nothing wrong with wanting an American education... or an English education from the UK, for that matter. The bottom line seems to be that if a Bahraini Arab has the opportunity for education, and studying in America is one of the available options, then absolutely. They'll go for it.

"If America is such a money hungry, immoral country, then why do the Bahrainis come here?" questioned American Karla Thompson.

"I agree," added Joan Corey. "It seems like Arabs trash us for our Western culture, yet they want it all... American-made automobiles, clothing, electronics, and computers..."

The Cultural Learning Curve

Mona Rashid Al Zayani, president of the Gulf University in Bahrain and a pioneering educationist, commented in an article on literacy in the September 8, 2007, *City Tribune,* saying, "The external outlook of literacy may see an increase, but if you look beneath the surface, the levels are only declining. As far as education for a purpose is concerned – high school graduation or college degree – we are seeing an upward trend, but gaining general knowledge toward culture-building is diminishing." She contended that there is no such thing as gender disparity in literacy rates in Bahrain evidenced by national high school results where the top eight students are invariably females.

A Bahraini mother told me, "As youngsters, both boys and girls should be encouraged to opt for any field of study that will enable them to take up a profession of their choice and grow up as well-educated adults who can stand on their own feet. Everyone, regardless of their sex and economic status, should have the opportunity for the best education at either affordable costs or free of cost. An educated woman is an asset to this society."

Girls enrolling in universities in the Kingdom registered a five percent increase over 2007, dispelling the myth that Arab women lag behind their global counterparts in the pursuit of education, according to the annual report of the World Economic Forum (WEF) in November 2007. The study assessed one hundred twenty-eight countries on how well they divided their resources and opportunities among male and female populations, regardless of the overall levels of the same resources and opportunities. The four areas of inequality between men and women the WEF examined were economic participation and opportunity, educational attainment, political empowerment, and health and survival.

The study concluded that within the past few decades, as a result of generous public spending on health and education, most Arab countries have dramatically improved the status of women. The rise in the average literacy rate was up to 52.5 percent in 2000 as compared to 16.6 in 1970, and in 2007 was at a reported eighty-four percent. At the same time, the report found that a wide gap still remained between the economic participation of men and women. Critics contend that these international surveys do not take into account the cultural differences of the countries they are assessing.

The study found that only thirty-one percent of Bahraini women work compared to eighty-nine percent of men, who also hold ninety percent of the positions, such as legislators, managers, and senior officials. In rebuttal to these findings, Dr. Yousef Mashal, Bahrain Export Development Society chairman, said, "Most of the jobs that are acceptable for Bahraini women within this culture are jobs that do not pay much money. But that does not mean good jobs are unavailable for them... the barriers are placed by women themselves, who cocoon themselves within the culture. They do not want to work in places where there are large numbers of men."

The schools in Bahrain have now opened up subjects for girls that once were only for boys, such as science and math, according to math teacher Wafaa Ashoor. "Yet there is technical high school for boys, but not for girls, such as, auto mechanic classes. It is still like that today.

"Maybe a year ago, women asked for a lady driver's education instructor for girls. Parents do not want their daughter taught by a man alone in a car. So now we have lady instructors. We also have lady taxi drivers, and private girl's schools have lady bus drivers."

A former Bahraini teacher explained that students were never encouraged to read books in school or at home, and no reading assignments, book reports or library visits were part of the curriculum in Bahrain's government schools. The private British and American school systems in Bahrain were the exception. Yet with Bahrain's emphasis on education and support toward post secondary education, both abroad and in the Kingdom, certainly there must be an abundance of required reading.

Abdulla al Sada, now retired, began his career as a teacher and rose through the ranks within the Ministry of Education. He has heard many educational viewpoints, yet has some misgivings about Bahrain's current educational system. "The new generation is really lost, I believe, because if you talk about education, that is not their main focus as a positive way to face the future. What is going on outside of the classroom is different. We are teaching things that are only informational. Our education system is not helping young people solve problems and use their minds independently. Listening to a teacher talk and memorizing things is not education. There are some things taught in the schools that are inaccurate, but the student has to write it that way for the exam. I think it is wrong to teach wrong information."

"If you ask a lot of college students, they will tell you that their first year of college was hell because they were not taught in the government schools to prepare for college," contended Lee Ann Fleetwood, the parent of five children. "College requires doing extra work, opening a book, working on research papers; they don't teach that in the government schools in Bahrain. A lot of kids who study abroad are totally out of their comfort zone. They either fail or call mom up and say 'bring me back home; I don't know what I'm doing.' It takes a very dedicated student to quickly learn how to do the job that the school system doesn't teach here; otherwise, they will fail. For those who do go abroad to study, many of them will pass and do a good job because their individual families probably encouraged reading at a young age. But as a whole, reading is not encouraged here."

Reading and literacy are not problems unique to Bahrain, or the Middle East for that matter. They are also a prominent issue in the United States. In November 2007, the National Endowment for the Arts (NEA) released its study results of U.S. reading habits, renewing the debate on literacy and learning among Americans. The bottom line results indicate that overall in all age groups, Americans are reading less. Statistics from the more than forty broad-based studies on various American age demographics all pointed to this. Nearly half of young American adults aged eighteen to twenty-four don't read books for pleasure, and a whopping fifty-eight percent of middle- and high-school aged students use other media, such as watching television and listening to music while doing homework. The NEA study proponents argue, "These negative trends have more than literary importance. They correlate, among other things, to fewer job opportunities, lost wages, higher incarceration rates, and less participation in civic and community life, including voting and volunteering."

Women's Rights

The status of women in all societies prior to Islam varied drastically; however, in general, women were degraded and viewed as objects of lust regardless of religious orientation. For example, under Babylonian law, as well as within the Greek and Roman civilizations, women were degraded and denied all rights. Early Egyptians considered women evil and "of the devil." Prior to Islam's spread into Arabia, Arabs looked down upon women, and it was not uncommon to bury alive a newborn female infant. It was men under the guise of their interpretation of God's will that removed equality and enslaved women. This is evident today with the way the Taliban treats women in Afghanistan.

Islam has always proclaimed a woman, whether single or married, as an individual in her own right, with the right to own and dispose of her property and earnings. The groom gives his bride a marriage dowry for her personal use, and she retains her family name, rather than taking her husband's.

Bahraini Muslim women have the same fundamental rights to life, education, profession, healthcare, justice, and choice as any Muslim man. Islam also gave Muslim women respect and honor. Yet there is open violation of all of these rights. Some Arab Muslim women told me that they feel many Muslim men have chosen to ignore women's rights in favor of their own ego-driven, patriarchal male code of superiority, as part of political Islam.

"Yes, women do have the right to divorce," Fleetwood commented, "But men take that right away by either using culture or the court system, leaving women in fear of losing their children and ending up with nothing. Their lives are controlled by the entire male population of the Muslim world."

Salah al Shuroogi stated that in the case of divorce, Sharia law says even if the Muslim father abused his son, but the mother is non-Muslim, the son (and all the children) must live with the father. "This will not be negotiated in the courts because it is one of the basics in our religion. Furthermore," he continued, "If an Arab man and non-Muslim woman are married, and the father is found to be abusive toward their children, the children will be sent to the father's mother to live, or to an aunt, if the grandmother has died."

The Bahrain legal system consists of Sharia (civilian) court and the high courts. The Sharia court passes a judgment, and one can appeal that judgment by taking it to the Constitutional court, which is similar to the U.S. Supreme Court.

I heard again and again that the sexes in Bahrain are equal but separate – not segregated – but separate. "The belief in the Muslim world is that women are equal as created by God, but we have our positions as well," Fleetwood alleged. "The men should have the superior position just by the fact that they are men. Based on the Quran, God says there is no difference between men and women; they are equal. And God doesn't judge us on gender, He judges us by our actions, and the way we live our lives. But the Arab culture, going way back, still views women as little more than property. God tried to change this thinking; women are not property, they are human beings. They are the other half of men. He said He created men and women to be with each other as equals. The Prophet tried to change that thinking also by setting the best example of treating women as human beings. Even his followers took issue with that. They objected to the Prophet's treating women as equals, and once the Prophet died, his followers began stripping away the rights of women."

AMERICAN Generalization #5

Muslim women are not treated equally with Muslim men, and do not have the same rights, particularly in the workplace and court system.

The reality in this Muslim country, from what I have seen, heard and read, is that there truly is a gap between women's rights and how women are treated. However, it would be inaccurate to portray all Bahraini Muslim women by the stereotypical image as ignorant, oppressed, and submissive. The generalization is not necessarily true, however, as it relates to the workplace.

"I believe that the thinking still persists today that the man is superior and the woman is inferior. That's one cultural aspect that has not changed that much in all these years," said Fleetwood. "The irony is that women have to fight for their rights in Muslim lands as well. Meanwhile, God gave them their rights; it's all there in the Quran. They shouldn't have to fight for anything. It should never have been taken away from them. And the fact that they have to fight for something that God himself gave to them is a shame."

Fleetwood and other Bahraini Muslim women pointed to the Hadith as the "offender." "Hadith says women are inferior intellectually and religiously, and more women will be in hell than men by the mere fact that they are women," explained Fleetwood. "The Christian concept of women is that because of Eve, women are cursed and the downfall of men. Now in the Quran, there is no such concept. In the Quran, women and men are equal. In Islam everybody is responsible for his or her own actions. But because so many Christians became Muslims in the early days of Islam, they brought that 'sin' of women with them, and that's where the inferior status of women crept into the Hadith so much. Already the Arabs thought little enough of women, and even though the Prophet changed it greatly, with all the influx of foreigners into Islam bringing their own beliefs about women, a lot of the Hadith sounds like it's almost straight from the Bible. There is nothing about the rib of Adam in the Quran; that concept came from the Christian Bible. Yet the Arabs believe that – they will tell you that women are made from men.

"I find it a shame that women have to fight for their rights. You should not have to fight for something that God gave you. And then when they do fight for it, the men call you a feminist like it's a dirty word or something."

Within the past few years, Bahraini women are more and more actively fighting for heightened rights – marriage rights, divorce rights, and child custody rights. Women want power and more say about their rights. Yet, as one Bahraini mother, who wished to remain anonymous, concluded, "Bahrain is an intensely patriarchal society that still promotes women as a lower gender to be covered up, bossed over, and subjugated. Children grow up seeing this and believe it's the norm."

Although both parents have the responsibility for teaching social and moral values, mothers need to be particularly proactive in this role, teaching their children not only what's right from wrong, but also that women are intelligent creatures with as much to offer society as their male counterparts. It's the only way to begin to change centuries-old, culturally-conditioned attitudes. Yes, that is a start, but it needs to advance further, and encompass genuine empowerment.

"The Quran says heaven is at the feet of your mother, and implores Muslims to respect their mothers," said Fleetwood. "It builds women up, and this Arab society tears women down. I tell my sons that when they marry, they need to respect their wives; your wife is a human being. And when they have daughters, they need to love them as well.

"The sexes are not equal in Bahrain. If a woman is showing her hair (or even if she isn't), if she's near a man (as in a few hundred meters), if she looks at him (as in glanced his way at some point), if she talks to him (as in asks for directions), then she more or less intruded on his space with her physical body, her voice, her smell, her presence – and to Arab men that means she is obviously not a good Muslim girl and, therefore, subject to male advances. Muslim women are blamed for immoral sexual behavior regardless of how that behavior came about – rape, sexual molestation as a child, from a boyfriend or stranger," Fleetwood continued. "The women are blamed, while the men involved walk free without blame."

According to Wafaa Ashoor, women can freely use the public buses for transportation, and the first few rows of seats behind the driver are reserved for them. "But I cannot be in a taxi alone with a man who is not my relative unless it is very important, and I am struggling to get some place. But, I could take a sister or girlfriend with me – constituting a group – as a man would not dare to try anything then."

In June 2007, Islamic scholars held a conference organized by the Justice Ministry's Religious Affairs Directorate. Shaikh Khalid bin Ali al Khalifa, the minister of Justice and Islamic Affairs, reported that the Islamic nation was going through a critical phase that required a watchful stance. "Given its rich, deep-rooted Islamic history," he told the press, "Bahrain has assumed a pivotal status in the Islamic world, which urges it to play a crucial role in pushing for a unity based on love, fraternity, and mutual respect." Shaikh Abdullah bin Khalid al Khalifa, president of the Supreme Council for Islamic Affairs, acknowledged that Bahrain was undergoing an exceptional period of freedom and openness, but chose not to elaborate.

Rasool Hassan said he feels that the Bahraini woman in today's society has succeeded in her quest for available career and job opportunities, such as doctors, lawyers, parliament members, saleswomen, professionals, and even private taxi drivers. "I think it is very open for women in Bahrain. Women are very ambitious, and they like to work. If you are a woman and you want a female taxi driver, you can call and request one. I think most women want a good education, and then to make something of that education. It is neither right nor wrong for women to work outside the home, even after having children. But I'll be very honest with you as a father and husband; I do not think it is right that the housemaid takes care of your kids. I think the couple needs a plan – and not many do – and agree beforehand on what is best for them. In my family, I work during the day and my wife watches our children. When I get home from work, she either goes to the university for evening classes or stays home and studies, and I watch our children. I find no problem with this. We have an understanding and it works. When she comes home from the university, we sit together and talk."

In the private sector workplace, according to Hameed Alawi, if a man and woman who both hold a master's degree in the same field are hired at the same time, with the same amount of experience, they will be paid the same. "We don't differentiate between the sexes, only between their experience and education."

Nader Shaheen also agreed that Bahraini women are treated equally in the workplace and paid the same given like educational backgrounds and experience. But perhaps this is more so for professional "white collar" female workers, he admitted.

Wafaa Ashoor disagreed. "Cultural equality here is improving. It's not everywhere, although we want to be equal with men. I am a teacher, and teachers do not receive the same pay. The male teachers do the same work as the ladies, and for the same number of hours, but the lady makes less."

"I worked for twenty years in the Ministry, and we never differentiated between men and women," Abdulla al Sada said. "The pay scale is the same; we have grades. The salary is based on the tasks and job description, not the person who is going to fill the position."

Not only does Mr. al Shuroogi believe that in most situations men and women are paid the same, but that they should also receive equal retirement payments and benefits. "We have the best pension system in the GCC; it is very good. But they need to do something about it for Muslim women. If a woman's father or husband dies, she will not get anything from his employer. If the man dies and he has a wife and children, immediately she will get back one eighth of his wealth. If he doesn't have children, she will receive half of his wealth. If he dies and his mother is still alive, she will get one sixteenth of his wealth."

Al Sada admitted that perhaps in the private sector there may be some positions or situations where men and women are not paid equally, but not in the government. "Labor laws, for example, impact equality. In some private sector jobs, the law does not allow girls or women to work at night. Additionally, Muslim women are expected to breastfeed their children until two years of age; therefore, working women have extended maternity leaves. In situations such as these, private sector employers may prefer men to women because men logically will work more than women."

Female union leaders from the General Federation of the Bahrain Trade Unions (GFBTU) claimed that lower wages and unequal treatment compared to male counterparts subjects many women workers to stress, making them less productive and compelling many to quit working. Ms. Saud Mubarak, head of the women's committee under the GFBTU, cited statistics of only twenty-five percent of Bahrain's local labor workforce as women, at a union conference in September 2007. "Many are afraid to join [the union], which shows they have less sense of freedom than their male counterparts," Ms. Mubarak told conference attendees. She cited lower-paying job sectors such as in factories, cottage industries, retail shops, tourism, and hospitality.

Call it a double standard or call it outright discrimination, in the Bahraini courts and legal system, women and men follow different rules. Hameed

Alawi cites an example: "Let's say I and a woman both saw someone breaking into a shop. A woman's account is not the same as mine. The police say they must see what she is like and review, review, and review. But if two men say they both saw the man break into the shop, their testimony is accepted without reviewing the case. The female witness requires either three or four other witnesses to corroborate her story."

"A hundred years ago maybe that was true," interjected al Shuroogi, "But not today. I do not believe there is any difference in our court system between men and women, even in the Sharia. One woman is enough to be a witness."

Empowerment

The constraints of culture lie within the community and the way the community and culture think, according to Nadia Alawi of Bahrain Women's Society. "It begins in the family, and with the new generation of children, and how they are being raised – that is the root cause."

Ms. Alawi cited a study on the perceptions about the roles of the sexes conducted with various groups of primary school children in an interview with the *GDN* in November 2007 during the third annual Arab Forum on Human Development. The children were told to pretend they were the opposite sex, and then asked how they would feel about that. Ms. Alawi reported that the girls said they were happy to be boys, because they now had the freedom to go out, whereas the boys said if they had to be a girl, they would feel like killing themselves because women always have to be supervised.

"This shows how the children have been raised. Women empowerment in the Arab world can be truly realized only if all stakeholders work together to change traditional perceptions about women in the community and at home," Ms. Alawi contended. "While new laws are needed, if we don't tackle the way culture perceives the role of women, they will not have the courage to strive for their rights. We aren't saying women have to work and leave the house, but the door must be opened for her so she can make her choice without the community's influence. As a human being, she has a choice."

According to Ms. Alawi, significant change in cultural perceptions will only come about through the work of governments, the private sector, non-governmental organizations, the media, educators, and others. She said that cultural perceptions about women are starting to change, but generally they remain only at the "theory" level.

Wafaa Ashoor said that women's empowerment is an important issue today in Bahrain. "There are many girls from my family and my husband's family running banks now, which is very good. Women are taking a position, and nobody is stopping them."

She reported that more than thirty-seven years ago her father passed away when she was twelve years old. Her mother stood up for herself – a testimony to empowerment.

"Everyone was asking her how she thought she could raise three girls on her own. 'It's not in our culture', they told her. 'Your husband died; you have to go back to your father.' My mother said no, she would live on her own, open her own shop, and support her daughters. That was 1970. My father left her a little bit of money to support us from his work. My mother, a housewife, had never finished high school; she had only gone through sixth or seventh grade. She knew she was good at sewing, needlework, and knitting. She got a machine, began making things, and selling them to ladies. She would stay up all night sewing. In a year or two, women were ordering dresses and things from her. Her embroidery shop is now the largest in Manama.

"So I grew up seeing my mother arguing with her family on how she would support herself, which was a big deal. They even stopped talking to her for a while. My mother was very strong, and proved to herself and her family that she did not need to depend on them, which was very contrary to the culture."

Gender discrimination in the workplace, the educational system, the legal framework, volunteer work, and the Arab culture are all contributing factors in a multi-layered cloak of discrimination, hindering empowerment of Bahraini women, claim the results of a study by the Bahrain Centre for Studies and Research conducted by activist Fayza Al Zayani and released in August 2007.

Other highlights of the study indicated that women faced many problems in higher education and vocational training, as university admission policies in some majors discriminated against women despite the known fact that female school graduates had a higher success ratio than their male student counterparts. "The bias is because the private sector intends to recruit men in scientific posts," Ms. Al Zayani said. She went on to criticize the Ministry of Education for allegedly assigning classes, such as textiles and housekeeping, to female students in secondary education and not allowing them to enroll in technical courses.

The WEF Gender Gap Index 2007 results, highlighted previously, also indicated that Bahraini women's political empowerment was among the lowest among countries surveyed, at just three percent.

Living in a deeply patriarchal culture, it's understandable why women have hesitated in the past to speak out against injustices they have endured over the generations. But if true women's rights and gender equality are ever to become a reality, Muslim women need to be heard, seen, and become active.

Rallying women to assume more public leadership positions is former United Nations General Assembly president Shaikha Haya bint Rashid Al Khalifa. But that's easier said than done when faced with thousands of years of cultural conditioning and religious interpretations. Shaikha Haya understands this, which is perhaps why she has been so vocal about stressing the importance of basing Islamic text interpretations to the needs of the twenty-first century.

"Often traditions are associated with religion, making them far more difficult to criticize or change," she told the *GDN* in June 2007, as she was about to finish her term as UN General Assembly president. "This has created a mentality that fears the autonomy of women because it is viewed as a threat, a threat to the traditional family, and a threat to marital relationships, as well as a catalyst to sexual freedom."

A powerful rallying call--invoking a powerful message. Will Muslim women respond? Will they view "sisters" involved in politics and public campaigns as threats to the Muslim society? A threat to the family unit? Will women continue to doubt their own skills, talents, and capabilities both physical and intellectual, and, as Shaikha Haya suggested, "accept a level of control and submission, even violence at times, to keep the family intact?"

Her view is that it starts with education that respects diversity and encourages critical thinking. As a first step, she challenged schools to implement a curriculum focusing on abstract subjects, such as philosophy and theology. "Subjects that lay the foundation to review, evaluate, and criticize the ideas that shape our societies," Shaikha Haya said. Citing recent Bahrain elections where numerous women ran for parliament only to be blockaded by religious leaders urging voters to not elect them, arguing that their place was in the home, she voiced her determination by responding, "We should not allow those who want to limit us to the past to solve problems of the present."

In the 2006 Bahrain general elections, eighteen women ran for parliament and municipality seats. Only one was elected, and that by default, as she had no opponent. It's a sad commentary that men refuse to acknowledge women as equal partners who can provide valuable contributions toward Bahrain's growth. This is an area where American women and Bahraini women share common ground. American women have been there before.

Shaikha Haya is not the only voice attempting to rally women in Bahrain to become active participants in the political decision-making process. Activists and organizations such as the Women's Union, the Supreme Council for Women, the Bahrain Women Association for Human Development, the Bahrain Women's Society, and others are blaming bias and discrimination against women as main stumbling blocks to women's empowerment, and calling for attention and demanding focus on this major issue. Numerous other Bahraini organizations have already launched empowerment campaigns.

In decision-making, the Bahrain government has attempted to empower women by appointing two female ministers and several women to top managerial posts in public organizations. There are now female judges, public prosecutors, and airline pilots. Women have been part of Bahrain's police force since 1970 when it became the first Arabic country to introduce female police officers. Political reforms have also contributed to empowering women in various sectors, especially granting them the right to vote and enjoy full political rights similar to male citizens. Women constitute forty-nine percent of Bahrain's population, according to Bahrain Human Rights Society deputy secretary-general Abdulla Al Derazi.

Khalifa bin Ahmed Al Dhahrani, speaker of the Chamber of Deputies, went on record calling on women's societies to communicate and coordinate with the legislative council, especially women on the Shura Council. He publicly praised these societies whose aim is to serve Bahraini women and increase their awareness about their rights and role in their families and country.

Businesses, including the United Nations Development Programme (UNDP) Bahrain, are also addressing gender issues and exploring how to narrow that gap. "The gender gap is still a concern in the Arab world," Ali Salman, UNDP program analyst said during a three-day workshop in September 2007. "There is a big difference between sex and gender. When you talk about sex, you are talking about biological differences, but gender is looking at the whole issue from a social, political, and societal point of view – with this you come up with the concept of gender mainstreaming. When we say, for example, that females can't be engineers or mechanics, it's a discriminating statement." The UNDP Bahrain is committed to achieving the goal of gender equality and women empowerment through mainstreaming gender in both its management practices and within its programs.

In other areas, religious scholars are called upon to educate the community on the differences between the teachings of the Quran and the Arab traditions that suppress women. Human development expert, Dr. Yasser Al Eiti, told a November 2007 audience in Bahrain at the Third Annual Arab Forum on Human Development that there is a widely held misunderstanding between Islamic teachings about women, and the traditions and customs in the Arab world. He called for religious and political reforms to aid in enhancing women's empowerment. "The reason why it is so difficult to empower women is because of cultural perceptions. The view of women in the Arab world comes from traditions and customs, so scholars should acknowledge the difference between religion and customs. Not allowing women in Saudi Arabia to drive a car is because of tradition, not religion," he said. "Not allowing women to work outside the house or participate in political life, again, are traditions. Society needs to support the government's efforts of empowering women, because the culture is not."

But how does one go about implementing this cultural attitude change, and where does one start? According to Dr. Al Eiti, the most appropriate group to educate society about the rights of women is religious scholars, followed by the government and non-governmental organizations. Al Eiti's suggested methods include lectures, the media, arts, and informational brochures and leaflets. It also begins in the home with educating young children.

» My understanding is that the United States is the system of government that is built on commercialization and monetarism. It is that which drives everything. «

Nader Shaheen

CHAPTER 6

Consumerism and Foreign Policy

In today's globally tech-savvy environment exploding in competition to be the first on the block to invent, produce, sell, and own the latest and greatest gadgets, American marketers and consumers are driven and focused on the future. Americans like to think they are near the top when it comes to being producers, whether that consists of technology or goods and services.

AMERICAN Generalization #6

Americans prefer to focus on the future, whereas Muslims seem to live in the past.

Absolutely Americans prefer to focus on the future. We are a young nation – a mere two hundred thirty-one years old – we're not old enough to have a past yet. America is still a land of opportunity. America and Americans have seen and experienced nothing but change from inception. We grow up believing that change is normal and expected. Life is constantly changing. When we point a finger toward the Arab world, it's from the perception that Arab societies remain constant. Cultural conditioning. You don't want to change; you don't want your culture to change. It is hard to change, but there doesn't have to be a conflict.

"Cultures change; that's what they do, otherwise we'd still be living in caves," stated Lee Ann Fleetwood. "People advance their thinking. They invent products to make life easier. But I don't see the Arabs doing that, and that's why they have become consumers and not producers anymore. The Arab world needs to catch up. This is 2007 but many of you think the same as you did one thousand years ago. You are not Bedouins any more."

America's cultural energy is the driving force behind America's quest for the future, Nader Shaheen stated. "It is not driven forward by its theological energy; by and large, this is culture only. And incidentally, Bahrainis view American ambitions as empirical, as evidenced by America's need for military buildup. But that's another story."

He takes issue with the second portion of the above generalization stating that Muslims do not live in the past. What they do, he says, is refer to Islamic text [Quran] to try and center one's self so as to reach some sense of "me" and where am I. What is my place in the universe? "There are simple instructions in the Quran -- nothing complex about it -- that tell us how to attain the simple way of life. And that helps keep me centered. There are many Muslims who are under no illusion that current Islam is ideal, because culture is as much an influence on people's lives as religion is."

"We depend on other family members," explained Wafaa Ashoor. "We don't do a lot of independent thinking. Instead, we say 'okay, my father will help me, or my grandfather will help me'. We don't plan ahead like the Americans do. The Americans plan everything; we don't do this."

"We are consumers, I think, rather than producers, because the education system has become weakened in the Arab societies," said Maryam al Sheroogi.

"And the money came suddenly," interjected Wafaa, referring to her country's discovery of oil in 1932.

"Maybe fifty years ago this statement was true," contended Salah al Shuroogi, "but not today. We are trying to catch up with the future. Educating children beyond high school is one way of catching up to the future. We look at our bright past, our goals, and we are proud of our doctors and scientists. We even have national days to celebrate our scientists and their achievements."

Prime Minister of Malaysia, Abdullah Ahmad Badawi, addressed this same generalization in an opinion piece in the *Gulf Financial Insider* February 2008 issue. He wrote: "In many cases, Muslim countries have fallen behind because they have rejected the pursuit of knowledge, a fundamental injunction of Islam. Some Muslims have closed their minds and allowed the weight of tradition and narrow religious interpretation to stifle inquiry and innovation. Limiting knowledge to religious matters and an overemphasis on rote learning extinguishes the spirit of discovery. This is a disservice to Islam. Similarly," he continued, "Muslims often forget that work is also a form of worship and that Islam calls for diligence and industry. If Muslims adhere to these values, then Islam presents itself as a progressive world view, one that in the modern day should be focused on the furthering of knowledge and the development of human capital."

"Bahrainis realize that most technology comes from the West, and we are eager to be better and advance by utilizing all of the technology available to us," said Rasool Hassan. "For example, for one hour stand outside a shop and observe the people with the latest cell phones, and yet they still want to buy a better one with more features, when what they have is quite adequate."

Most of the Bahrainis I spoke with agreed that embracing new technology was a way to move forward and modernize, but they also emphasized that this is not the same as to Westernize. Yes, they want to incorporate the best aspects of Western civilization and technology, but within their own religious framework and cultural traditions.

An entirely different side to the issue of whether or not Muslims live in the past was indirectly addressed in a paper entitled "Global Intelligence Briefing" presented in early 2007 by Herb Meyer[2] at the World Economic Forum in Davos, Switzerland, and attended by most of the CEO's from all the major international corporations. In Meyers' opinion, there are four major transformations shaping political, economic and world events, all of which influence American business leaders and owners, culture, and the American way of life. One of these is the war in Iraq and how it relates to Islam and radical Islamism.

[2]Meyer served during the Reagan administration as special assistant to the Director of Central Intelligence and Vice Chairman of the CIA's National Intelligence Council. In these positions, he managed production of the U. S. National Intelligence Estimates and other top-secret projections for the President and his national security advisers.

In his paper, Meyer stated, "There is a radical streak within Islam. When the radicals are in charge, Islam attacks Western civilization. Islam first attacked Western civilization in the seventh century, and later in the sixteenth and seventeenth centuries. By 1683, the Muslims (Turks from the Ottoman Empire) were literally at the gates of Vienna. It was in Vienna that the climactic battle between Islam and Western civilization took place. The West won and went forward. Islam lost and went backward. Interestingly, the date of that battle was September 11. Since them, Islam has not found a way to reconcile with the modern world.

"People can argue about whether the war in Iraq is right or wrong. However, the underlying strategy behind the war is to use our military to remove the radicals from power and give the moderates a chance. Our hope is that, over time, the moderates will find a way to bring Islam forward into the twenty-first century. That's what our involvement in Iraq and Afghanistan is all about. That's why we have thought that if we could knock out the radicals and give the moderates a chance to hold power, they might find a way to reconcile Islam with the modern world. So when looking at Afghanistan or Iraq, it's important to look for any signs that they are modernizing.

"For example, women entering the work force and colleges in Afghanistan is good. The Iraqis stumbling toward a constitution is good. People can argue about what the U.S. is doing and how we're doing it, but anything that suggests Islam is finding its way forward is good."

AMERICAN Generalization #7

All Arabs living in oil-producing countries are rich.

Nothing could be further from the truth said Shaheen. "Before the discovery of oil (in 1932), we had fish, pearl diving, dates, and agriculture as our major source of economy. There were few affluent people here. Even in the 1970s, people here were mostly in the same class and struggling, but it was then that the rich Arab thing started. That's when the media showed Arabs acting ridiculous in casinos, but this was just a handful of rich Arabs. That perception has tainted the entire Arab world. Only in the '80s did you start to see merchant classes emerging, with people trying to do business and bring more money into the system."

Although class division became more prominent after the discovery of oil, some individuals I spoke with believed that, prior to this, there were affluent controlling families, families working in the market as traders, and those who were laborers, and that Bahrain always had rich and poor families. Others described the class divisions as being pearl divers and farmers.

"The average salary here in Bahrain is under two hundred dinars ($532) a month, but they are trying to raise it to two hundred fifty dinars ($665) a month," Shaheen stated. "Bahrain's cost of living is very high. Everything is so expensive, because it's all imported. Anything in a tin gets shipped in from abroad."

In Bahrain, the reality is that most young married couples are strapped financially, particularly if they own or rent a flat and are not living with family. Housing is expensive, and sometimes a couple cannot afford to live alone. Most new couples starting out are in debt just from the expenses of their weddings and furnishing their homes.

"We are only producing a small amount of oil in Bahrain," al Shuroogi told me. "It's something like one hundred thousand barrels a day, which is nothing compared to our neighbors. Bahrainis are working everywhere – in the petrol stations, restaurants, as taxi drivers... We have to depend on ourselves here, and we have to work hard. Even in Saudi Arabia and Qatar, nobody is rich other than old families that had wealth a long time ago. But ninety percent of the Bahraini population is working hard to earn money."

ARAB Generalization #6

Americans are overly concerned with money and profitability.

Remember the enemy: ignorance? People tend to generalize out of ignorance. Not all Americans are concerned with money and profitability, obviously. Nevertheless, Americans live in a system where it costs money to be part of the society. Paying taxes and health insurance requires money; so too does feeding and clothing a family. In the current economy, the American dollar is losing its value abroad. Bahrainis know this all too well, as their currency is pegged to the American dollar. So, if the above statement is within the context of struggling to make a living and providing for a family in a shrinking economy, then yes, Americans are overly concerned with money. American businesses may be overly concerned with profitability but--to say that all Americans as individuals are--is not a fair statement.

"The Americans that I have met in my life have been generous people and haven't had much," Shaheen told me. "They also haven't been particularly well off, and haven't really wanted any more. I don't see greed in America in the same way that I see greed here in Bahrain. The Arabs can be really greedy. Never mind our reputation of being generous; yes, we are generous. But I've met some really, really greedy Arabs."

ARAB Generalization #7

Americans are very good at giving money for humanitarian efforts, but they are also very good at killing people.

"Interesting," mused Shaheen. "Actually, as a percentage of your GDP (Gross Domestic Product), Americans are the smallest donators in the industrialized, developed world. You have the highest percentage of your budget on arms and the lowest in charitable donations. It looks big in terms of volume, but the percentage of your population is low."

Addressing the second part of the generalization, Shaheen said, "My understanding is that the United States is the system of government that is built on commercialization and monetarism. It is that which drives everything. If anything, it has nothing to do with the balance of the guilt; rather, it's where is there a profit? And I'm talking about corporate America – the corporate decision makers – not people in jobs.

"Corporate America, the military, and the ruling elite of the U.S. are who do pretty much everything. Also, no debt relief ... the U.S. will not provide debt relief to anyone. 'You owe us money; so keep paying.'

"I think people have to understand that in the Arab world, Arabs are very, very different than Americans," he emphasized. "Everybody, unfortunately, is being dragged along in the same boat. And no, I don't believe that Americans are trying to find a balance for their guilt."

Hameed Alawi acknowledged hearing and reading in the media about the United States providing money for humanitarian causes, and he is not surprised. Bahrainis hear good things about America and its citizens. "There are good things; nobody can argue that," he said. "But they [United States through its military] are killing people, and this is the argument. Most of the people in Bahrain will tell you that America is trying to create a balance."

"Everyone gives money in America," said al Shuroogi. "The individuals, the actors, the companies. This shows that Americans are good people. We never had a problem with American people; it's with the politicians only. Even Bahrain gave money to the Katrina victims. After the Katrina disaster, I believe the United States will accept any help from any country. Whenever there is a natural disaster somewhere in the world, the first people to give aid are Americans and then the Saudis. The Saudis bring medicine and food. They will give to anybody, not just Muslims."

"It's happening on both sides. It is only a skewed view of the world that these people have who believe this generalization," asserted Shaikh Ahmed bin Isa bin Khalifa al Khalifa, assistant undersecretary of Nationality, Passports and Residence. "Unfortunately, people are good at passing out blame, but they're not good or as fast coming up with solutions. Unfortunately by nature, Bahrainis come up with blame more than with solutions. You would see something that somebody did, and they would not commend him for his efforts, the first thing they would say is this is bad. ... It's skewed. I don't know what the solution is. Maybe it's me taking my kids to the States every other year and giving them a broader understanding of America and Americans."

Americans I spoke with disagreed with this generalization, pointing out that the individuals who give their money toward humanitarian efforts, be it supporting breast cancer research, flood, fire, or tsunami victims, or local animal shelters, are not the ones who are killing, and vice versa.

ARAB Generalization #8

The American government has created problems in the world just to have power and political clout worldwide. America can't be trusted.

"Created?" questioned Shaheen. "No, they've capitalized on problems in the world. In many ways you are victims of circumstance. Everybody was in favor of the U.S., and massively pro-U.S., because they opposed the Soviet Union, who was also hell bent on world domination. It's just that the typical Russian way of accomplishing that was with massacre and murder. In the vacuum of there being no Soviet Union, the U.S. has this very large army that has to be kept busy. It does have a rule of its own. It does have lobby powers of its own, and it is very formidable. You are the U.S. military with your Air Force, Army, Navy, and Marines. That position is an enormously powerful one. Keep them fighting, and keep them busy, and keep them working. War is profitable. I think that has had more to do with it than political clout."

"From my position, Americans are good people," Hameed Alawi observed. "It's the American government that I'm concerned about. The government is trying to gain power worldwide and not let anyone share with them. They want to be on the top always and keep other countries subservient. Your American government does not reflect the American population. It is the government's policy and not what the people want."

Ali, who did not want to use his last name, said, "The greed for power has blinded the U.S. They no longer fight for justice; they only fight for power and control."

"I believe this statement is one hundred percent true," agreed Wafaa Ashoor. "America does it just to show they are strong. That is how you show your strength; you invade countries. The price is very steep, of course, when losing your soldiers. What I see in politics is the American government saying one thing to the Israeli group and something different to the Palestinians, and nobody trusts each other. Who's running it? America. You cannot take the word from the American government. This is my opinion," she concluded.

"Oh, what a joke," exclaimed American Michelle LaGue in response to the above generalization. "Yeah, we created the problems in the Middle East. They've been fighting since before we were a country. We're trying to save them!"

Minnesotan Joan Corey offered her opinion as a spirited discussion began among seven American female friends. "I think the government does have a motive in mind about what places they are going to enter. There is a reason, and it's not always in the best interest of the people who we, as Americans, think we are helping. The U.S. may go in with that intention, but we end up just hurting the people of those countries. You can't just throw money at things and think problems are going to be resolved."

"It's possible though that the oil countries where the U.S. has gone into are the most corrupt because they do have the oil and they do have power," added LaGue. "The oil actually makes them corrupt, which is why they have treated their people the way they have. That's why we try to intervene."

"Look at Sudan," continued Corey. "They are a very poor country. Look at the way they treat their people. Why are we not all upset about that? I think our [American] perception is that our government thinks it's not worth it."

"I don't think it's not worth it," countered Karla Thompson. "I think you can't go into every country. They [American government] need to ask themselves what action is going to have the most impact on us."

"Look at Afghanistan," interjected LaGue. "We have been in that country forever. How much oil and money do they have? And all because of the civil war there. I don't think Afghanistan has any oil, do they? Case in point right there."

"But that's where Al Qaeda is," replied Corey. "And we've got to get Al Qaeda. We trained bin Laden and financed Saddam Hussein. Hello!"

"And they both got powerful and corrupt," added LaGue. "Any time any one person has so much power, they become corrupt. It just worsened with those two; we created two monsters."

Once Saddam Hussein blatantly ignored the U.S. government's demands, he became a liability and the U.S. wanted him removed. And this is exactly the Bahraini Arabs' point: It's the American government's fault, because we created that monster.

"We did create the monster," admitted LaGue, "But we didn't know it. We had the best intentions. I think we learned not to contribute to someone so much that they gain so much power."

"And we're probably still doing it, and we [citizens] don't even know about it," stated Sandy Meyer.

From my discussions with Bahrainis, I came away with that exact sentiment. The average American does not really know what their government is doing.

"That's why we have a different president and Congress every four years," added LaGue. "We need those checks and balances. Our government can't get too corrupt, because we do have so many checks and balances."

The War in Iraq

Prior to the U.S.-led invasion of Iraq on March 20, 2003, Washington unsuccessfully lobbied the UN Security Council for a second resolution paving the way for military action against Iraq if Saddam Hussein failed to comply with demands to disarm.

Since the invasion, Iraq has plunged into chaos and overlapping civil strife that has divided its rival religious and ethnic communities and left tens of thousands of civilians dead. The Shiite parties suspect Sunni leaders, who were loyal to former dictator Saddam Hussein, of supporting violent insurgent groups. In return, the Sunni leaders have accused the Shiites of conspiring with neighboring Iran in attacking Sunni civilians. Widespread sectarian violence is believed to have increased in February 2006 with the attack on a Shia shrine in Samarra. By late summer of 2007, tribal leaders who had allied themselves with the United States to fight Al Qaeda in Iraq were being methodically kidnapped. Relatives of one of the abducted Shiite sheikhs blamed Sunni extremists and said the attackers chose a Shiite neighborhood to stage the kidnapping to create strife between Shiite and Sunni tribes that had united against Al Qaeda. The abductions highlighted the shifting nature of the conflict to infighting between Sunni and Shia groups, who are increasingly targeting members of their own sects who align themselves with U.S. forces.

Nearly two million Iraqis have fled their homes for other parts of Iraq since the invasion, according to a report issued by Iraq's Red Crescent Society. That figure does not include the two million others, as estimated by the United States, who have left the country completely.

Those in Bahrain with whom I discussed current world events, as well as a majority of Americans I spoke with in the Midwest, opposed the invasion of Iraq except for one man -- Nate, an Iraqi. I met Nate one evening in a hotel lounge in Bahrain. He told me that he was a former Iraqi translator for the U.S. troops in Baghdad's heavily fortified Green Zone. After nearly a year and a half – and refusing to wear a mask – his identity was discovered. He subsequently sent his family to Syria for their safety, and he fled to Bahrain in search of a job. He believes that the U.S. did the right thing when it invaded his homeland, and that the war was justified. His only regret was the length of time he put his life on the line for the benefit of the United States government's military and, in the end, he was denied a visa to bring himself and his family to the U.S. where they might begin a new life.

In the current political climate, it takes a brave American to admit that his nation just might have gotten it wrong.

Headlines have glared for months in both the U.S. and abroad that George Bush's plunging popularity ratings are a direct result of his ordering the United States to war. The *Star Tribune* Minnesota Poll, released on October 3, 2007, indicated that sixty-five percent of Minnesotans polled were pessimistic about the state of the nation and unhappy with President Bush. "Much of the bad feeling appears tied to displeasure with President Bush, whose job approval rating has sunk to thirty percent among Minnesotans – the lowest level yet recorded by the poll," surveyors said. Furthermore, according to the poll results, only one in four Minnesotans felt the nation was going in the right direction, whereas in 2000, more than sixty percent of Minnesotans thought the nation was on the right track. The poll admitted that at least some of the despondency about national affairs in 2007 springs from growing fears about an unsteady economy.

Tension between the Muslim world and the U.S., in addition to other Western countries, has been dangerously high since the horrific terrorist attacks of 9/11. With the U.S.-led invasion of Iraq, the news is dominated by violence and body counts. The Bahrainis I interviewed voiced very strong, and sometimes angry, opinions about the United States government, its president, and its foreign policy, yet none showed any hostility or unfriendliness toward me as an individual, knowing full well that I am an American.

"We are mad at the Americans because of their government and what it does," said Rasool Hassan. "They do stupid things, and I don't know what for. Just for power, I guess. To be honest, I'm really scared for tomorrow's future, for our new generation. I don't know how we are going to explain this to them. It is very complicated. If one of my sons comes to me and asks what has happened in Iraq, what do I tell him? Should I really tell him what's happening? If I do, believe me, he will start hating the Americans."

"But, in fact," he continued, "When we sit with Americans and get to know them outside of America, we don't believe they are bad. They are really very nice people, very gentle and helpful. I don't understand. Sometimes I ask myself if Bush and Clinton are really American. Personally, I think the reason behind this is all politics and power. The Bushes and Clintons and others are people who have the money, and therefore, the power. I definitely believe that a lot of Bahrainis feel the same as I do about this. There are no other reasons. What if tomorrow America says, you Bahraini Arabs can go to hell; we will not support you? We would go back centuries. That's why I told you that I am personally eager to be better than America or anybody as a Bahraini, because I'm married to this country, and I'm proud to be Bahraini.

"In Iraq, the American government was wrong. Where is the nuclear bomb; the weapons of mass destruction? Believe me, the American government has created problems, and I believe the American government is going to make this gap that we're talking about bigger, and bigger, and bigger. I think they will create enemies not only for the American government, but unfortunately, also create enemies for Americans."

"I don't think Americans are here to promote democracy anymore," Al Jamri explained. "They are here basically to preserve status quo. And they got rid of a naughty individual – Saddam Hussein. But I think long-term we will only have a better place for peace or prosperity.

"Our people have nothing against Americans. If we have a democratic environment, if justice for Palestinians is established, if the bias toward Israel is stopped or contained, then there are all the possibilities available for better peace. I don't think it's far off. You could establish a better environment easily where American interests are secured anyway. They don't have to overdo it.

"Again you could see the same story of Al Qaeda and Taliban in Afghanistan repeating itself with Saddam in Iraq. The same group supported it all. Saddam became too powerful later on, and he started to behave outside the limits allowed him, and so he had to be crossed out. I'm anti Saddam and I hate bin Laden. I hate terrorists, but it is the Americans who were backing these people in the first place. And the same story repeats itself all the time.

"This hypocrisy is not portrayed properly, or is not described, and that's what creates all this confusion. We see lots of it here since we're on the receiving end of it," Al Jamri concluded.

Hameed Alawi also explained that much of the political talk in Bahrain about the Sunnis and Shia fighting each other in Iraq is considered directly related to America's doing; setting these groups up to fight with each other. "Think of these two groups fighting each other and do not think of what the U.S. is doing for a minute. It's like the American government has devised this plan for Iraq – and other countries – to get them to fight each other; using them as a weapon, but in a different way. In the meantime, the Iraqis aren't seeing that the U.S. is stealing their oil. America wants the oil, and that is why America does not want to leave Iraq. They [American government] are drawing their attention away from U.S. policies and the real reason why they are in Iraq. And then they make deals with them [Iraq government], such as forming an American military inside their countries to 'save' them from other countries and sell them weapons.

"There is political talk here about America causing a problem between Iraq and Kuwait, for example. Why?" he asked. "Because they want to take advantage of selling Kuwait's equipment, of taking their army base and getting an advantage of having the money. Kuwait will say okay, but then you must give us something in return. And they make an agreement. This is why we say that America gains advantage in the world by causing problems.

"In the Gulf region, the American government did this by selling Gulf countries weapons, their armies, and fueling demonstrations. We didn't have armies before, just small military groups. But ten years ago, we had a lot of disagreement about creating big armies in Bahrain and Qatar. Qatar didn't have anything before then; now the biggest space in the Gulf area is Qatar. In Bahrain, we have a large army base, boats, and lots of weapons. We don't need these. We are a small island; we will die in a minute. It is clear to the Bahraini people that America is just playing this game to gain advantage over us.

"We know America is taking advantage. For a long time, we knew nothing about you. People here think there was an agreement between Saddam Hussein and the American government. For example, the first war was with Iraq. America felt Iraq was getting strong, so they sent Saddam Hussein to fight for Iraq. Saddam was very weak but supported by America, and even Bahrain. It was all planned.

"People here hate the American government, but feel differently toward the American civilians. We all hate bin Laden. He is not a real Muslim. He is from a very small sect of Islam that was divided later on. These terrorists take advantage of Islam and try to destroy ... some people say bin Laden was doing a lot of business with the U.S. government and had its cooperation, but then something happened. Nobody knows what that was.

"It is the American government's policy to cause wars, but it's not what the American people want," professed Alawi.

Shahzada Wazir voiced his opinion about the U.S. government in a letter to the *GDN* in June 2007, writing, "The U.S. and Britain became killers of innocent children in Afghanistan and Iraq for promoting a Jewish global agenda across Muslim countries. They sowed the seeds of hate, bias, and prejudice between Muslims and the West. Now they both are considered as occupying nations of Muslims' resources.They tarnished the image of Islam and became the real imperialist powers of the twenty-first century."

"President Bush managed to convince his countrymen that Saddam Hussein was a criminal and intent upon destroying the world. That he had stacks of weaponry capable of mass destruction and was a threat that had to be wiped out," wrote Bahraini Mohammed Ali. "No evidence was found of any such stockpile, and so many hundreds of thousands of people have been killed since then with no let up in sight."

Bush has been labeled a hypocrite in the international media, and there are plenty of Bahrainis and expatriates alike in total agreement with that view. Expat Rory E. Morty, who lives in Bahrain, had this to say about George Bush when Bush delivered his address at the UN General Assembly in late 2007: "He [U.S. president George W. Bush] attempted to adopt a platform of human rights in his address to the UN General Assembly. This is the same president who has illegally invaded a country without UN sanction, for entirely political motives, and in doing so has killed hundreds of thousands of civilians, not to mention American soldiers, and deliberately misled his own people.

"This is the same president who supports torture and 'extraordinary rendition'--a horrendous process of detention without trial, with the specific aim of exporting these prisoners to countries with poor human rights records so that they can be 'legally' mistreated. This is the same president who actively blocks the unrestricted access of the International Committee of the Red Cross to prisoners detained at Guantanamo Bay! Is anybody else utterly exasperated at the raw hypocrisy of Bush? His speech was an insult to the UN."

"I'm willing to bet you that before this war started, even before the Gulf War started, that you could point to any American and ask them to locate Iraq – or the Middle East for that matter – on a map, and they couldn't," Lee Ann Fleetwood challenged. "They might find Israel, but other than that, Americans have no clue. Then suddenly Iraq is in the news every day and what are you seeing? People killing people. And what the Americans don't seem to realize is everything that is going on right now is going on because America went over there and caused it. For sure Saddam Hussein was a dictator and murderer – there's no doubt about that. But Americans seem to forget who put him there. Who gave him the money? The WMDs that Bush was looking for? Guess what? Bush's daddy is the one who gave them to him. And so we go and give it to Saddam back in the '80s, then come back in the late '90s and demand them back. When Saddam used the chemical bomb on the Kurds, America didn't care. The American government didn't do anything. Saddam killed a hundred thousand or so people, and it barely makes the news in the U.S. But then he goes to the border of Kuwait and suddenly the U.S. is over there fighting a war. You can kill people in your own country, just don't go to another country and do it.

"Arabs feel that Americans are hypocrites because we choose our battles depending on the benefit for us," she continued. "If Saddam is killing Kurdish people, well, who in the hell are the Kurds? We don't give a damn about them. That has nothing to do with us. But when he got greedy and wanted Kuwait; now he's posing a threat, and not only with Kuwait, but also with Saudi on the other border. Now what's in Saudi that the American government wants? Oil. If Saddam Hussein gets his hands on oil, then what?

"Bahrainis are very proud people, and they find at this time that America has become the bully of the planet," contended Fleetwood. "We will force our way if not given it. We will force our way on your people. Even Americans are realizing this. Nobody likes a bully.

"Unfortunately, this is something very true in every country of the Arab world that is run by a king, a military dictator. There is no freedom of the people. They cannot express their anger about being ruled by a greedy king or a bloody military coup leader. They can't express that without putting themselves in danger. So if you can't express your anger to the ruler of your own country, then the next best thing is to point that anger at someone who rules another country that is open to anybody. America right now, because of what they have been doing in the world today, is the target of immense anger. That's a safe way to direct your anger because you can't point it at your own king or dictator for fear of being put in jail or facing retaliation.

"Something I realize about Arabs," she continued, "is that they don't like to accept blame for things. Everything bad that happens to Arabs happens because of someone else. With the situation they are in today in the world, I don't think there is anything Arabs accept – it's what everybody else did to the Arabs."

"The problem is if you don't have the power, and you don't have the money, you can't do anything," said Maryam al Sheroogi. "Who else besides America? America is the emperor of the world. We are angry at America because of what is happening in Iraq. We are angry with them because of what they did to Iraq. It makes us sad because we like Americans. We are angry with the Americans because they didn't do anything. All we hear is that George Bush must be good because this is his second term as president. If the people didn't want him, they would not have voted him in again. The Arabs will not accept that Americans do not approve of Bush and what he is doing in Iraq. George Bush has become a curse for his country. We Arabs are sad, and we are mad."

In response to the comment that the majority of Americans must approve of Bush since they elected him to a second term, Michelle LaGue offered a rebuttal. "The only thing that we can do is be accountable to who we vote for. That's our voice and our responsibility. The media is going to report what they report, but at least if we have decent people in office... We do not understand whom we are voting for because we don't take the time to learn about the candidates. As responsible citizens, we must know the candidates' platform and hold them accountable."

"Even if you do vote for somebody, just because the government makes a decision doesn't mean you necessarily agree with that decision," pointed out Karla Thompson.

"And don't forget about the huge majority of Americans who are so apathetic that they won't even vote," added Joan Corey. "There will never be an issue that you will agree one hundred percent with a candidate on. It's never going to be a perfect system."

"There may be the president with his agenda, but then you have the House and Senate, and they differ," added Jayne Dietz.

"As long as we have the checks and balances, and the ability to vote, it will work," said LaGue. "But people have to take more time to become more informed and involved. There's so much information out there on the Internet. But I'm the first to admit it; I don't take the time to learn."

"Your government says bin Laden caused this, but bin Laden is not in an Arab country," pointed out Mrs. al Sheroogi. "He is in Afghanistan. So why not search for bin Laden and kill him if he is a terrorist? What he did was against the Islamic religion. Our religion is for pacifists. Our religion is not about killing people. So why didn't the American government go looking for bin Laden? Instead they went back to Iraq.

"The problem is what happened in Guantanamo, and what happened at Abu Graib prison. Arabs are now doing what Americans are doing. Your people! For us, they are one and the same. We blame the Americans for what they are doing in Arab states; they destroyed Iraq. They destroyed its heritage. It's not only a country; it's a heritage. Who is to blame for that? Bin Laden? No, it's the government of America. Instead of going after bin Laden and kicking his ass, they came back to Iraq and killed innocent people. And what's happening now? The Iraqis are killing each other."

"The problem I have with that," interjected Fleetwood, "Although she is right, is what are the Arabs doing rather than complaining, shaking their fists, and burning American flags? What are the Arabs doing to help the situation?

"If you go into a government school today in Bahrain, you will see the Jewish and American flags on the floor so that students can walk on them," she disclosed. "My children get upset because they are torn between it.

They are Arab, they are Muslim, and they are American. So they go to school and see students stepping on the American flag. Now the flag to them is not that special because they haven't been to an American school or raised in America. But having an American mother, I'm special to them, and the flag is special to me. So they feel guilty or torn about what they should do as Arabs, and what they should do as Muslims, and what they should do about having an American mother. I find it ridiculous actually. Yes, I love the flag of my country, and I respect it, and would never do anything like that. But it does not bother me in the least if somebody else wants to burn it or step on it. In the end, it's just a piece of cloth.

"Arabs will find that the American government is difficult," contended Fleetwood. "You rarely heard the word 'terrorist' ten years ago. 'Fundamentalist' was a term usually associated with religion. The word 'jihad' had never been heard until the Iraq war. That word is so blown out of context! Now when Americans turn on the TV, every night you can find a newscast using the words 'terrorist, suicide bombings, jihad' – all of these words inflame listeners, which they are meant to do.

"Every time George Bush gives a speech, the word 'terrorist' is thrown in there regardless if it has anything to do with what he's talking about – find a way to put it in because they want that word to be constantly in the American mind. There is a 'terrorist threat' out there. I'm saving you from it by going to them, and getting rid of that threat rather than letting them come to our soil.

"There are rulers in countries around the globe killing their people as we speak – in Rwanda, Sudan – hundreds of thousands of people being murdered daily. I don't see the government of America on their borders ready to take charge over the situation. There are countries all over the world where dictators are killing people, and those countries don't even make the news.

"We call it genocide when people are killed within a country, and that's an internal matter that we don't need to deal with. What the American government really means is there's nothing in Sudan that they need, so let the Sudanese deal with it.

"When Saddam was killing the Kurds, they didn't threaten us in any way, shift the power, or break any deals we [America] had with Saddam, so we let him be and do what he wanted. But as soon as he got greedy and wanted to expand his power into Kuwait, well then, our benefit was threatened. So now we have to take control away from Saddam Hussein. And that's how and why Bahraini Arabs see America as hypocrites – when there is a benefit for you as a government, and you ignore everything else."

Albert Diaz disagreed with the popular Middle East opinion that America has an envy of Middle Eastern countries and their natural resources, and that the American consumer is greedy and allows elected government officials to involve America in wars to satisfy their greed. "America was not at war with any Middle Eastern country when a suicide bomber killed more than two hundred Marines in the bombing of their barracks in Lebanon on October 23, 1983. The United States was not at war when terrorists attacked our country on September 11, 2001, killing thousands of Americans. Furthermore, I do not see special shipments of oil arriving in America as a reward for getting rid of a dictator [Saddam Hussein] and oppressive regimes. If we went to war for oil, why are gas prices now over three dollars per gallon in the U.S.? If the U.S. is envious of Middle Eastern countries and their natural resources, then why do the oil-rich kingdoms and countries in the Middle East continue to amass great wealth from oil sales to all countries, not just the U.S.? Regarding the U.S. presence in the Middle East, I wonder how many Iraqis would rather have the Saddam Hussein regime in power. Would the Kurds feel safe again in Iraq or would they be afraid of another chemical attack from their great leader? Would women in Afghanistan rather have the Taliban in power or have the opportunity to attend school and receive an education? How can a war end when insurgents continue to flood these two countries to disrupt the peace and prosperity that the citizens want?"

By May 2008, the death count of U.S. military in Iraq had surpassed four thousand.

Despite the vocal attacks from Bahrainis, a vast majority does not believe the world is locked into a "clash of civilizations" that will lead to violent conflict between Islam and the West. At least that is the finding of the

British Broadcasting Corp. World Service poll[3] results released in 2007. The more than twenty-eight thousand people surveyed found that fifty-six percent believed that common ground could be found between Muslims and Westerners, while only twenty-eight percent felt violence was inevitable. A breakdown of the key results indicated:

- Fifty-eight percent blamed tensions on intolerant minorities, not cultural groups as a whole. But twenty-six percent identified fundamental differences between the cultures as the root cause.
- In the United States, sixty-four percent believed in common ground, but thirty-one percent saw conflict as inevitable.
- Overall, fifty-two percent of the five thousand Muslims surveyed said common ground was possible, including majorities in Lebanon (sixty-eight percent) and Egypt (fifty-four percent).
- Only in Indonesia did a majority – fifty-one percent – think that violence was inevitable.

President George W. Bush Visits Bahrain

President George W. Bush's historic visit to the Middle East, and more specifically, to the Kingdom of Bahrain on January 12-13, 2008, marked the first time a U.S. president visited Bahrain. It also presented an ideal opportunity for the two countries to address misunderstandings that might exist, and to build bridges for the future with Arab leaders.

It is believed in the Middle East that the U.S. aims to dominate the world – their exact words. It is also assumed that we in the United States are against Islam. Although I personally believe both of these generalizations are incorrect, it is very difficult to dissuade the Bahraini Arab Muslims of their steadfast positions. I do believe, however, that it is true that the U.S. has a serious interest in the Middle East.

I was in Bahrain during the president's visit. He acknowledged the shared

[3]The poll was conducted from November 2006 to mid-January 2007 by the polling firm, GlobeScan, and the Program on International Policy Attitudes at the University of Maryland (wwwglobescan.com/news_archives/bbciswest).

vision both countries have about the Middle East's future and their continued strong alliance. His Majesty King Hamad told the Bahrain press, "We share the U.S. president's view that democracy is the sole way to defeat terror, extremism, and radicalism". He also stressed that Mr. Bush's visit would produce a positive impact on regional peace and stability--efforts Bahrain intended to support.

The Kingdom of Bahrain honored the president with a red carpet welcome although President Bush did not appear in public during his brief stay.

Those Bahrainis and expats on the street who welcomed the president's visit nonetheless felt it should have come years earlier. In general though, he is extremely unpopular there, and his visit was greeted with bitterness, distrust, and scattered demonstrations, predominantly as a result of the prolonged war in Iraq. There remains a high mistrust of the American government from the average citizen on the street. Their sentiment toward Mr. Bush's visit seemed unanimous: "Stop the war and give us [Middle East] peace." Obviously, easier said than done.

However, if the war sentiment could be put aside with at least some open-mindedness and a lot less angry emotion, it could lead to the start of a new beginning of understanding and tolerance on the part of the Bahrainis. Afterall, most Bahrainis can identify many things about America that they like.

The Israeli-Palestinian Divide

The State of Israel was created in 1948 out of the Nazi Holocaust at the end of World War II in 1945. Its Arab neighbors have despised the new nation since its inception. They have refused to recognize Israel's right to exist or to accept the United Nation's promised homeland for the displaced native Palestinians. The UN created a plan to partition Palestine into two nations, one for Jews and one for Arabs. Jerusalem was to be designated an international city under UN control. Most Jews reluctantly accepted the plan, while the Palestinians flatly rejected it. The loss of Palestine became a volatile symbol of the humiliation of the Muslim world at the hands of the Western powers. Peace has been a tenuous illusion ever since.

With a population of more than six million, three major religions claim Israel as their holy land: Jews, who comprise eighty percent of the population, eighteen percent Muslims [mostly Sunni] and two percent Christians.

The Six-Day War of 1967 was Israel's defining moment. Not only did they triple their landmass, but also they found themselves with millions of hostile Arabs living in the West Bank and Gaza. The Israelis have fought their neighbors for decades ever since, struggling to survive.

There are four major issues dividing the Israelis and Palestinians: borders of a Palestinian state, Jerusalem, Palestinian refugees, and West Bank Jewish settlements.

AMERICAN Generalization #8

Arab Muslims hate Israelis.

Yeah, pretty much true, the Bahraini Arabs tell me. But it isn't all the Arabs hating Israel; it's all Muslims. And yet there is no Islamic reason for this, according to Nader Shaheen. "This is a five thousand-year-old argument dating back to David and Goliath. The Israelis are in a country that isn't theirs, and speaking a language that isn't theirs.

"Actually, it's a posse of Zionism that is the biggest Arab thorn, the Zionist policies and Zionist expansion policy. Not that the Arabs have a problem with Zionists being the Nation of Israel with its core of Jews expanding outwards," Shaheen said, "but the expansionist political belief. It's Zionism that does that.

"The Arabs feel in many cases that the Israelis are like the abused child that has now gone on to abuse, which is an unpopular thing to say, but it's true. It's also true to say the Arabs have never persecuted the Jews. A big war, but never persecuted them; not like the Brits who kicked them out, or the Germans who did it more efficiently than anybody else, or the French who kicked them out, or the white middle-class Bible Belt Americans who certainly made no buts about attacking them, and who still hold the Israelis, I believe, and the Jews responsible for the death of Christ. You can find extreme reasons for the most stupid things in the world.

"So yes, there is some truth in the comment that Arabs hate Israelis. But it has to do with the inequality of the way Palestinians were treated. In truth though, it's a real estate argument that has been going on for five thousand years that has nothing to do with me as a Bahraini. Do I feel hatred toward the Israelis? Not really. Do I feel sympathy toward the Palestinians? Absolutely. Do I think they should have a homeland? For certain. Do I think there should be a wall in that country dividing them? Absolutely not.

"It's amazing how the language of the Israeli press from the government has changed. Now it's not a Palestinian nuisance; now it's their 'war on terror.' What's the likelihood? You are the chosen people, no question! Palestinians have legitimate gripes, but because we are on the tail end of the world's sympathy scale these days, they aren't going to get anything at the moment. We need to try to engender and develop sympathy for our experience. With everyone thinking that we are rich, that won't happen. Lots of money is not a subject that's guaranteed to get you much sympathy. True or not. That we are religious extremists is also not a subject guaranteed to get you any sympathy from the world; although it's not true.

"A blurry line for most Arabs relates to what the difference is between the two nations of Israel and Palestine. Not for the first or last time have the Americans used Israeli secret service to perform various acts of territorial violation whether it's Syria, Iran, or Iraq. So I think the Arabs' view is quite right; let's not be playing ball here."

"I will tell you something," said Salah al Shuroogi. "The Israelis are Christians, and the Christians said no one is allowed to visit Jerusalem. What do you want us to say? Can you differentiate between the Jews and the Zionist party? Did you know that there are some Jews who are members of the Palestinian parliament? Deseminarian Jews we call them. And then there are the socialist Jews. What do they want? They want one nation. And the United States is also asking for one nation. But one nation is a separate nation. The Minister of Foreign Affairs is an Arab, and a Palestinian Jew. They can live together, but your media will not tell you this."

"The State of Israel is portrayed in the West as the only democratic country in the Middle East," contended Al Jamri. "In fact," he added, "it is only democratic for Jewish people amongst themselves. But this is the only country that says they own the land because God told them so. They say they have the right to do what they do because God told them. Where is the democracy in this?

"Bin Laden is killing Americans because God told him to. And bin Laden has killed Soviets because he said God told him to. Israelis are saying that God said in the Torah that this is their land, and therefore, they should take it. Where is the democracy in that? Bin Laden is saying that God told him as well. So what's the difference?

"We have the Palestinian people who are demanding their rights," he continued. "The Palestinian Arabs are prevented from returning to their homes, which is a reversal of the Declaration of Human Rights. The Americans support the Israeli side. Why would the Americans support a non-human rights practice? Why would the American administration support a non-democratic state when somebody tells it that God told them, and then we have to believe that?

"We believe that the American people are really good people. I have only respect for Americans; for their kindness, for their lightheartedness, for the jokes they tell as they live, for the way they work so hard, and for how intelligent they are. Yet the average American doesn't know what his administration is doing. He doesn't know anything about the Near East Policy. There is no policy about the Middle East that would be allowed to permeate without being filtered by the Jewish lobby. There is nothing allowed related to the Middle East. Any person must pledge loyalty to the State of Israel before pledging loyalty to the Constitution of the United States of America.

"To be allowed to function in presidential campaigns, you need money from fundraisers, many of which are Jewish," continued Al Jamri. "And so the American system is well paid by the Jewish lobby. It's got nothing to do with the American people.

"The media is really biased. They don't tell you the story of Palestine, and therefore, this is where the Puritan salifists say, look, this is the biggest, arrogant power, supporting a bunch of Israelis who say that God said this is their land.

"What we see, as Arabs, is a total bias toward Israel that is creating anti-American feeling. This is undemocratic. Israel says God told them this is their land. Okay, so what's the difference? Bin Laden says God told him to kill Soviets, and now God told him to kill Americans. What's the difference between the two?

"What we see here in the Middle East is this contradiction. I believe that the American government has lost its convincing power; they cannot convince us. Understand that it is very easy to create anti-American feelings amongst people who see the contradiction from here in Bahrain and other Gulf countries.

"Arab people cannot understand this undemocratic policy. There is no democracy whatsoever. Israel took this land from the Palestinians, and why? Because God told you to take the land? And then the Americans have to support Israel on this.

"Well, sorry. Because there's Al Qaeda, which is antithesis. Al Qaeda is there; it's just the other way around basically. I'm not saying that the Israelis have to get out, or that they don't have a right to exist, but this principal of what's been forced onto everybody in the Middle East is very unfair.

"Now that brings you to the nuclear issue. America is currently very anti-Iran because Iran MIGHT have a nuclear power, a nuclear weapon. Okay, we're all against nuclear weapons. But the Israelis had one hundred twenty nuclear warheads in 1984, according to one of their own scientists. God knows how many more there are now. Nothing whatsoever is said about Israel having a nuclear armament that they could use to destroy everybody. Why? Can you explain it to an average Arab? Why would the average Arab believe the Americans?

"These contradictions create anti-American feelings. But it's not only Americans, because people love to eat at McDonalds, they love to wear jeans. Even hijab ladies wear jeans. They love American places, the movies, and American music. Arabs would love to go to American universities; they would love to live in America, as well, because American people are great. It's hard to find an American person that you hate; they are so kind and nice. You are not dull and boring people. But, as for the American policy toward the Middle East, as for their wrongdoings in Afghanistan creating the Taliban, helping even to create Al Qaeda, and then see what that led to..." his voice trailed off, then he said, "Well, people can see these things, but not absorb and buy into this."

Hameed Alawi said he thinks all Middle East countries disapprove of Israel. "Israel is occupying Islamic land. Israel wasn't even a country; it was just a group of people. They got quick money and support from the U.S. since the U.S. wanted to get rid of them from inside their country. They were kicked out of different European countries. The Israelis have caused a lot of problems. They have caused war, and they have killed men, women, and children."

What does it take to set past differences aside and move forward? "There have been problems for more than fifty years," Alawi said, sidestepping my question, "and they cannot live in peace. For example, there are a lot of foreigners who live in the U.S., but they have certain procedures for nationality that they must follow, and do follow, plus they respect the U.S. government. But the Israelis want to live in Palestine while showing the Palestinians no respect."

Wafaa Ashoor cited a recent situation to explain her position about Israel. "My son applied three months ago at various shops and companies for a sales position. One company replied very quickly, so he went to work for them. Yesterday another company called to interview him, and when he told me the name of the company, I immediately said they were Israeli. I told him I preferred that he not interview there, because a long time ago I had read in the newspaper that the owner of this store sends part of his store's profit to the Israeli government. It's not that he is Jewish," emphasized Mrs. Ashoor. "I like Jewish people. There are lots of Bahraini Jewish people here. It has nothing to do with the religion or the people; they are very nice. But the Israeli government is what I don't like."

ARAB Generalization #9

Every decision made by the American government is made with Israel's benefit in mind. The American government is highly influenced by Israel.

"As it pertains to the Middle East, yes," agreed Michelle LaGue, as a reaction to this Arab generalization. "But they won't recognize that they [Israelis] are people. They won't give the Israelis the acknowledgment that they should exist. They don't think Israelis should exist at all. They need to accept that there are Israelis, and they should just get over it."

Sarah Miller disagreed. "It's hard to say that they should get over it by now. Would you get over it if you lived there, and someone came in and said get out?"

"Would someone tell me why they allowed Israel to put up a wall?" asked Joan Corey. "They took it down in Berlin. Why is the American government here not completely upset with Israel for putting up that wall? I'm upset about it. I don't think they should have done it. And they [Israel] are kicking people out of certain areas, telling them they can't live here anymore. America can't control everything. And we don't want to. It's not like we were the British going into every country that we wanted and taking it over."

"We do not run any country outside of our borders, and never have," LaGue stated.

"Talk about having someone's benefit in mind; we're changing our laws in the States because of the Muslim religion. Airports now have to have prayer rooms and washing areas," Corey interjected.

LaGue agreed, saying, "The problem is when we can't have Christmas trees up in certain areas, or anything associated with Christianity, yet we have to add areas for Muslims to say their prayers."

"Our lawmakers are doing this because they are afraid of getting sued. We are a sue-happy country," added Corey.

"The perfect example is the imams at our airport who were kept off the plane because they were kneeling and praying in public and have now sued Minnesota," LaGue said. "It made national news. What's going on in Minnesota? They think we are totally leftist liberals because we're now accommodating Muslims. That's the reason we have prayer areas and sinks for them to wash in. It's because they are suing us and saying that we are discriminating against their religion if we don't provide these."

"On the other hand, anyone who goes to Utah and is not Mormon is going to feel the isolation from the Mormons. And the Amish people within the United States live within their own pockets of areas and do not change their religious or cultural practices. They have their own communities," said Corey.

Maryam al Sheroogi contended, "America says that we are the dog's tail of Israel. But every decision the American government makes about Israel is to benefit Israel and not anything else. That's a huge view here.

"My dad had two Jewish friends here in Bahrain whom he did business with. In 1981 and '82, there was talk of hate toward the Jews," she continued. "When I was eight years old, I remember people asking my dad why he talked to these Jews. 'Their people are killing Palestinians. Why do you talk and eat with people who kill your blood?' That's when I started turning against the Jews. I think it is the Arab culture that is pushing these views about the Israelis. I remember teachers in school telling us that the Israelis were bad. I think part of it is the sensitive relation between the Arabs and Jews. Their culture and our culture pushed them apart. Muslims and Christians are more alike than Muslims and Jews. Now that I am older," she admitted, "I understand that I don't hate Jews; I hate the Israeli government policy."

Wafaa Ashoor added, "The few Jewish Israeli individuals who are billionaires are the ones running the government, supporting the elections, and everything else over there. At least this is what we hear and see in Bahrain."

As another international peace initiative conference neared in the Middle East in November 2007, His Majesty the King, Hamad bin Isa Al Khalifa of

Bahrain, announced that the Palestine issue was at the core of the Middle East peace process, and ensuring that the Palestinians enjoy their rights was vital for long-lasting peace in the region. The Kingdom's diplomatic position on the Palestine cause is that "Bahrain will always participate in any international initiative to further the cause of the Palestinians, a common factor for all Arab and Islamic nations. This also underlines the importance of peaceful moves to solve the Palestine issue and support the Palestinian people in achieving their rights, and establishing an independent state with Jerusalem as its capitol, and the return of refugees, according to UN Resolutions 242, 338, and 194."

Presenting an open-minded view of the Israel-Palestinian divide was Xerxes, who chose to withhold his last name. "Peace talks with the Israelis should be encouraged at every level," he said. "We all understand that the vast majority of Arabs are uncomfortable with Israel's behavior (and not without cause) and even with its very existence. However, the practical reality is that Israel exists, and it has the backing of a significant military power. It is in everyone's interest for there to be a dialogue, even if the prospects for solutions seem remote.

"The alternative," he continued, "is to condemn future generations on both sides to ongoing hatred and bloodshed. Hate eats up the hater; it doesn't just hurt the hated. The only way forward is an agreed-upon two-state solution. People, of whatever religion or political persuasion, want peace... more than anything."

September 11, 2001

We weep and mourn, yet are sobered and determined.
Although we have been knocked back onto our heels,
together as a nation, we will rise upon the wings of eagles.

Anonymous

The American homeland came under assault on September 11, 2001, as nineteen Middle Eastern militant Muslims under direct orders of Osama bin Laden and Al Qaeda, the terrorist organization bin Laden created, hijacked four jets and launched a surprise attack. Two of the jet airliners flew directly into the World Trade Center in Manhattan, one barreled into the Pentagon, and the last slammed into a Pennsylvania farm field (instead of a building, thanks to the heroic efforts of passengers on board). In all, 2,973 innocent American civilians lost their lives, not to mention those of other countries who were in the World Trade Center towers, the Pentagon, or on either of the three airliners. President George W. Bush addressed a stunned nation on television, proclaiming the attacks as "acts of war." In the wake of this tragedy, the American government entered into a new type of battle that Bush coined "the war on terrorism." His battle cry to rally the shocked and grieving American people was, "Whether we bring our enemies to justice or bring justice to our enemies, justice will be done."

The United States was not at war with any country when attacked by the Muslim terrorists.

"This man bin Laden, who is he, really?" asked Abdulla al Sada. "This man who has frightened the United States has no knowledge; he has nothing – Bedouin bin Laden. Yet he is controlling the entire world with advanced explosive technology."

"Had the United States after 9/11 resolved to establish peace in the world, and sent out a pulse of peace with as much massive financial resources that it could call on, it would have advanced the American dream by one hundred years," asserted Shaheen. "It would have ensured continued success of America in its own image. People would have flocked to that. That is infinitely more attractive than the incredible advances in various ways that you can annihilate each other. And that was just ignored, because the Bushes want to push it this way. News is unfolding at a more rapid pace than at any time in the recorded history of humans because we can contact each other immediately. We have access to communication immediately. Ten minutes ago a plane hit the World Trade Center; now everyone in the world can watch it live.

"The one thing we know about empires is that they do ultimately collapse. In the United States, I think it will begin with a deep cessation from the union.

California itself has the seventh largest economy in the world. It doesn't need to be a part of the Union. And that, in my opinion, is how it will unfold when it does. The only certainty between communications these days is that it will happen much faster. Because of that, it seems to me, an imperative that whenever there is sympathy toward you in the world, and you capitalize on it in the most benevolent way – you spread your schools, you spread your money, you build institutions – the American Institute of this and the American Institute of that – and teach the whole world how you do things, that for me is a much more preferable model for an empire. And it is easy to sustain and much more lasting. There was a time of 'Americanesse' when people aspired to that. Nowadays that isn't the case in the world.

"Instead, there was an enormous opportunity in favor of militarism. The benevolence that might cause the economy to suffer a bit, although it would come back, wasn't fifteen percent a year, which is your ratio on General Dynamics, Boeing, and the Arms, which are kicking back fifteen to twenty percent. Thank goodness there's a war! That's where your president wants to be. That's the American hoe the road system. War is profitable. In politics, they've all got their own versions of bribery and corruption.

"But here we're also subjected to real punitive KYC (know your customer) within the banks under the umbrella of financing Islamic terrorists through the financial system," continued the Bahraini bank vice president. "Don't forget the two largest Al Qaeda accounts were HSBC London and Citibank Dubai, and no one talks about that. If I'm an Islamic terrorist, I'm not going to hide my money in an Islamic bank, am I? I want to hide it somewhere where there are well over three-and-a-half-million account holders; they'll never find it. That is where, if you are going to hide your money, you will hide it – in the open.

"And here's another thing that has never been addressed. I think it's amazing that a military the size of the U.S. with over five hundred thousand soldiers, not including the Reserves they could call up, would only commit seven thousand soldiers to search for Public Enemy Number One – Osama bin Laden. How can you commit only seven thousand troops to that? How desperately do you want to find him? I'd have stuck one hundred thousand men searching for him – no stone unturned and no turn un-stoned. I'd search everywhere. So to commit seven thousand Special Forces when it's not even a case of Special Forces; it's just people on the ground... Go and find bin Laden; look everywhere. If your president would have done that, I think you would have found him.

"That raises a lot of questions among those of us who have studied the United States and watch closely, because if you do something, it affects us. If you don't do something, it affects us. So a real sensitivity to the fact, and a real knowledge of what influence America imposes on the rest of the world, is something I don't think past presidents, and certainly not this one, have really understood."

Shaikh Ahmed bin Isa bin Khalifa al Khalifa offered his point of view: "I think after 9/11 America drew a road map that was supposed to be the definitive answer to all the problems. The road map was based upon certain things that needed to happen within a country in order to get it to the desired level. But you cannot place a square peg in a round hole. I think the American road map based its premise on that if you democratize all of these parts of the world where problems are, the problems will cease, and power to the people will be restored, and all that good stuff... The Arab world is not built around that.

"Our society is different. Children don't leave. Families are the most important part of society. It's something that needs to be given some time, reach an understanding – it's eventual – but it needs time. I think the American government's road map wanted some definite and quick results in order to get things done. This then created a lot of confusion.

"Religion is part of our life. Religion comes first," continued Shaikh Ahmed. "We cannot, no matter what anyone tells you from this part of the world, divide religion from culture, politics, and law. Its part of it, and it cannot be separated. The premise of democratizing and exchanging the ways of our society into something similar to the West is creating a lot of confusion for these people, and that's something you don't want to happen. But it was something that I think people back in the States saw as the answer when they drew this map. In any plan or path that you take, there are deviations and corrections for these deviations. Then you get back to the path that you wanted to be on. So hopefully, both sides have understood that, and adjustments are made in order to move forward.

"I can sympathize about what happened on 9/11," Shaikh Ahmed went on, "But not what the Americans are doing afterwards. If something happened on my soil, I would go out and try to find who did it. If you were the biggest kid on the block and suddenly you are walking in the crowd and get slapped real hard, you go looking for somebody. How can you explain it? Sometimes irrational thoughts overtake rational thinking, and you might take actions that you might regret somehow. But then again, there's this 'shake it up and see what happens' kind of thing. It's affecting us, yes, but if we start pounding heads, we won't get anywhere. It will just get worse. It's a sad state of affairs to reach that point and end people's live in that manner. It's sad, and you see it across the news. It's happening in Lebanon and in Iran. It's very sad. The region hasn't seen so much economic boom and so much tension at the same time. It's unbelievable. The U.S. repatriated a lot of money back to the region after 9/11 – a lot of money. At the same time, you have this tension that is broadening and broadening. Hopefully common sense will prevail, and this is not going to come to a boiling pot with one country going belly up."

AMERICAN Generalization #9

Before 9/11, the Middle East seemed to be in another time. We never saw anything but camels and desert. After 9/11, nineteen terrorists became the face of the entire Arab world.

"Before 9/11, the Middle East seemed like a foreign movie without any in-depth personalities to connect with," explained Minnesotan Kathy Hanlin. "We didn't have any connection and, therefore, little or no understanding of what their every day life was like. I am sure that many Muslims can understand then why misconceptions about them and their religion would be prevalent after 9/11.

"Because I don't know and have never had any contact with anyone from Bahrain, or anywhere in the Middle East for that matter, my only information about the Arabs is what I get from the media," she admitted.

Another Minnesotan, who wished to remain anonymous, explained her feelings. "We don't see the common, every day middle-class Bahraini Arab. The only way we have to gain knowledge about them is from the high-profile incidents that are almost always bad. We need to know that Arabs love their children the same as we do. Of course, not all of them are suicide bombers and radicals, but that is what we are led to believe. Even the media has tried to point this out, although not often enough. We cannot learn from the extremists, and that is about all we have to base our feelings on. Just having Muslims run for office in our country is a good first step. We need to know these people on a more personal basis."

"Americans are curious about us," said Rugayah Sharif, "Partly because they have not been exposed to the Arab world. I have a friend from the university who went abroad to study. She wears a headscarf and wore it while there. Because people – and not just Americans – don't know anything about our culture, and because of the events of 9/11, they concluded that okay, she's an Arab, and so she must also be a terrorist. She told me about a time she was walking down the street, minding her own business, when a woman with a child walking in her direction came upon her. The woman told the child loud enough for my friend to easily hear, 'she's a terrorist; stay away from her.'

"Honestly, there are people who still believe that because of how the media shows Iraq and its people, and how we Arabs are depicted in movies as backwards...it's like we still live in tents in the desert and ride camels."

"You can only blame the media from both sides for that," stated Wafaa Ashoor in response to the above generalization. "The American media is not showing everything. When we went to the States in 1995, and again in 1999, no one we spoke with knew about Bahrain. They know Saudi Arabia and Kuwait, but not Bahrain. It's not a big deal to me. But we should not blame a group as a whole."

"I bet Americans don't know that Bahrain is the only country in the Middle East that has the Formula One circuit," ventured Nofa al Sulaiti. "A lot of people come here for the circuit as it's the only one in the Middle East. The Formula One is a very large, expensive event, and it is very difficult to put on. But as you see, Americans may know about the Formula One, but they have no idea that Bahrain is able to host this kind of massive event."

» It's hard to form an honest opinion about the Arab people when all you hear is what the media wants you to hear. «

Toni Grundstrom

CHAPTER 7

Separating Fact From Fiction

The power of the media is substantial, particularly as an agenda setter. The power of persuasion is probably the most essential element in influencing public opinion, something all public relations specialists know well. There have been plenty of books written on the enormous power of advertising, for example, as a persuasive medium. There are also those critics who contend that when personal involvement in an issue is low, so too is the interest in what the media is saying. When personal involvement and interest are both high, people take note of what is said and written in the media.

Everyone is biased. No two people perceive a message identically. Personal biases are nurtured by many factors, including stereotypes, semantics (key phrases or words), peer group pressures, and – especially in today's culture – the media. Media bias is rampant and evident in all forms: electronic, written, film, and audio.

Does the media have a social responsibility to state the truth and nothing but the truth? Is there a hidden agenda? Does the media purposely show death and destruction to sell newspapers and gain network television ratings? Is it a fallback to the early 1900s and sensationalism because that's what sells? Do people really want to read about this?

What type of role can the public relations industry within today's technologically savvy world play to combat media bias?

Media Bias

On a political level, women's rights activists went on record in Bahrain in mid-November 2007 calling for a public relations offensive against what they termed the negative portrayal of Arab women in the mainstream Western media. Shaikha Sabeeka bint Ibrahim al Khalifa, wife of His Majesty King Hamad and chairwoman of the Arab Women's Organization (AWO), said that the AWO wanted to work toward changing that negative perception. While admitting that women in the Arab world do face unique challenges, she explained to a *Gulf Daily News* reporter that Western media tended to only focus on the negative, while ignoring many positive stories. She called on governments and non-governmental organizations to work together to highlight positive issues concerning women in Arab countries.

"We all agree that we need to convey to the rest of the world the reality of the situation in our countries," she said. "In order to do this, we need to work together to ensure that the media highlights positive events and the achievements of successful women whether in the realms of scientific research or successful businesses."

The Arab and Islamic cultures have become much more defensive due to a perceived need to verbally defend themselves in the media. Arabs feel under attack by the "West," particularly with issues such as the 9/11 attacks on the United States. Because there is so much ignorance – true ignorance – in the world today between Arab Muslims and Americans and their government, the Arabs find themselves in a most uncomfortable place when constantly having to defend who they are and what their religion is about.

"One thing you will hear about the media in America is that when they show things about Muslims on TV, they tend to be really negative things," said Lee Ann Fleetwood. "They show you the negative cultural aspects of Arabs. Because they happen to be Muslims, people assume that this is the Muslim culture. But it is not; it is the Arab culture that you are seeing.

"Something I noticed while watching the news in America," she continued, "was how glorified the Vietnam War was. There was nothing left to the imagination. The war came into your living room, and you saw everything. On the other hand, the Iraq war is a big secret. All the Americans know about it is what the government decides to tell them via the media. More than four thousand Americans have been killed, but that's all you hear – the number of casualties. America may be the land of the free, with freedom of speech, but only as long as that speech is not pointing its finger at the government. Americans know nothing about the Iraq war. I think the Americans are misled.

"The Internet has really been an eye opener for anyone who cares to spend a few hours on the computer," she went on. "Of course, you can't believe everything you read, but that's true for newspapers and television coverage, too. At the same time, there is a lot of truth out there, and more Americans are opening their eyes and searching the Internet for it, rather than waiting for the evening television to show it to them. As an American Muslim living in Bahrain, I can tell you that the Iraq war is a huge issue in how the Arabs feel about the Americans."

ARAB Generalization #10

The American media shows and tells Americans only what the media wants them to know.

The above generalization, to a large degree, is accurate. The American media influences our opinions.

"You watch the Fox news channel and they tell you what they want," explained Wafaa Ashoor. "Then you listen to ABC, and you hear something different. You can tell the difference."

"I think we have all learned to take everything we hear with a grain of salt," said American Michelle LaGue. "If you are proactive, and you really want to know the real story, you can find it out."

Joan Corey agreed. "The same thing can be said for newspapers. Certain newspapers are more politically leaning toward one type versus the other, as are most television news stations."

"A lot of Americans I've talked to view Iraq as a backward country and believe America is there to liberate them, give them democracy, and bring them into the twenty-first century," asserted Lee Ann Fleetwood. "The way the media shows Iraq, or any Arab country for that matter, to America is as if they are living one thousand years ago. They don't show the modern skyscrapers in Baghdad; they show the poverty. They don't want Americans to see that Baghdad was already in the twenty-first century and even ahead of other countries. When they interview an Iraqi, it's always through an interpreter even if that Iraqi individual is a professional and speaks English. Americans don't know that Iraqi women had more rights than a lot of other women in the Gulf. Iraqi girls were going to school before a lot of them in other Arab countries. Iraqi women were working and enjoying having their money and education. Healthcare in Iraq was so much better than in a lot of other Gulf region countries.

"America is so ignorant of Arabs. It's because the news they show about Arabs and Muslims in America is as though the very worst information they can find was sought and then put out there in the media. And that's what Americans are fed daily – the worst bits of information available," Fleetwood stated. "And so that's what they think of Muslim Arabs. The American media shows Arabs either shouting death to America at the cameras or portraying them as extreme. They don't show the middle-of-the-road Arab."

Maryam al Sheroogi concurred with Ms. Fleetwood's assessment of the American media, adding, "The American media talks about everything going on in the Gulf, but there is nothing about what's really happened in Iraq. Do you remember when your president ordered the 2001 bombing of the building alleged to be a weapons factory? It turned out to be a milk factory. I bet the American media never mentioned how many people got cancer as a result of that bombing or how many diseases there are now. It's not only anger that Muslims have about Bush and the war in Iraq, but also the diseases. My brother-in-law is an administrator at King Faisal Specialist Hospital in Saudi Arabia. He has told me about the large numbers of Iraqis at his hospital complaining about the pollution. Why? And the handicapped kids being born. Why? And the numbers who have developed cancer. Why? It's because the government of America destroyed the land and buildings with their bombs that also caused disease. But the Western world doesn't know that, and certainly not the Americans. How do you think the rest of the world would react?"

In October 2007, a Reuters report out of Baghdad indicated that more than five hundred new cases of cholera had been confirmed in Kirkuk that week, bringing the total number across Iraq to more than three thousand. The newspaper article reported that fifteen people at that time had died from the disease, a low death toll, indicating that the outbreak was under control. A Ministry spokeswoman blamed the outbreak on poor water supplies in Kirkuk that had been bombed.

"I've noticed that the American media is more moderate," Fleetwood observed. "When you turn on the news and hear any kind of speech from a Muslim, whether a talk show or news clip, nine times out of ten it is going to be an extreme Muslim shouting jihad. 'Death to the government! George Bush is a terrorist.' That's what the media feeds Americans because that's what they want you to think of Muslims – that Muslims want death to all Americans.

"There are two million Muslims living in America. By and large they are moderate Muslims. There's also a huge influx of Muslims, but also a large number of American Muslims in America who have moderate views, live the Quran as well as they can, and certainly don't want all the Americans dead. It is their country, and they are proud of it just like anybody else. But you don't see these Muslims on TV.

"I was talking to this American Muslim who said she and her family were coming out of the mosque from Friday prayer with a lot of other Muslims. The local news station was there and wanted to do an interview. She said that most of the Muslims there did not have beards and were wearing jeans and T-shirts. Yet this American camera crew passed up every single one of the American Muslims and went straight to this guy who had a long beard, turban on his head, and dressed in a short thoub. He didn't even look American. This is whom they want to talk to, because that's what Americans think Muslims look like. She also told me that the camera crew wanted to interview women as well. Some women were wearing hijab and others weren't. One of the cameramen approached her (she was not wearing hijab) and asked her if she knew the name of a particular girl he was pointing out with the hijab on. The woman told me that the cameraman never saw her as someone to talk to because she had removed her headscarf as soon as she came out of the mosque. Instead, he wanted to talk to a hijab girl because that's who Americans identify as Muslims."

"So the media is spoon-feeding Americans," continued Fleetwood. "They tell you exactly what they want you to know about Muslims. The only view Americans get of Muslims really is of hard-core extremist Muslims who hate Americans. People don't normally believe everything they see on TV but, by God, they'll turn the TV on and believe everything they see on it about these Muslims."

"Al Jazeera News opened our eyes to the real information about the war," interjected Maryam al Sheroogi. "It boils our blood when we see the truth. But Al Jazeera is not just one station. We have Al Jazeera Sports, Al Jazeera documentaries, Al Jazeera Children, Al Jazeera Life, and Al Jazeera English. I think Al Jazeera is so much honest for us." [Al Jazeera is Qatar-based.]

"When I watch the news in Bahrain and then watch the American news, I would have to say that the news from this side is more truthful about what's going on than what the news from America is saying," said Fleetwood. "American news is very sanitized from the American side. Of course, it's biased here to the Arab point of view, but they will show more things and say more things on Al Jazeera. In my opinion, the American government doesn't like Al Jazeera, because Al Jazeera will show things that the American government doesn't want Americans to know about.

"If Americans would protest that," contended Fleetwood, "And if the Americans want to know what's really happening, they need to find out for themselves. The Internet has news shows. The government isn't going to give it to you if they don't want you to have it. So if the American government says that Al Jazeera television promotes terrorism, then by God that should be reason enough to get satellite and watch Al Jazeera. Let Americans make up their own minds.

"If Al Jazeera is truly a terrorist news station, let Americans watch it. Aren't Americans intelligent enough to make that decision? America is like a nation of children; the government has to tell us what we are allowed to see and what we're not. But aren't we the most free country in the world? Then suddenly Big Brother is right there to tell you that you can't watch such and such. Americans should be angry with that. I feel as though the American government is suddenly trying to take everything the Americans struggled for since becoming a nation out of our hands, and tell us they know what is better for us. The American government's attitude toward its citizens is 'calm down, sit down, watch your Hollywood movies, and leave politics to us.'"

"Something I don't understand," raised Michelle LaGue, "is why Al Jazeera allows bin Laden's videotapes to be shown, when all he is, is a terrorist giving the different terrorist cells instructions. I know there is freedom of the press, but the media needs to take some accountability when dealing with a terrorist. That is probably the biggest thing that bothers me. They put those tapes out there, knowing that bin Laden's whole purpose is to communicate to his cells. And after Al Jazeera shows it, every American television station shows clips of it."

"The point they are trying to make," countered Joan Corey, "Is the more people they can kill, maim and injure, or bring fear to, the stronger the message. Generally, they are going to go into a different area than their own people live. If they are Sunni, they will infiltrate a Shia area. Just like in Israel. The Palestinians can't move around the Israelis. The differences between Sunni and Shia are so few, it's like are you a Wal-Mart shopper or a Target shopper."

From a Bahraini Arab Muslim perspective however, the differences between the Bahraini Sunni and Shia are significant. It would be difficult to find a Bahraini Muslim to tell you that the differences are so minor that they could be compared to a Wal-Mart or Target shopper.

"And we've all heard that it's been like that in the Middle East forever and ever; why would we think that we could possibly change it now?" asked Sandy Meyer.

"There had to be some other form of government than a total dictator like Saddam who killed whomever he wanted every day of the week. That's what we (United States) tried to change. We don't want to change the Arab culture," emphasized LaGue.

Bahraini Rania Noor also weighed in on media bias: "We would be glad and happier if the Western media acknowledged the advancements in the Arab world. Sadly, these advancements are often overlooked by the West, particularly by the media that tends to favor unrealistic and stereotypical images of Arab women. We do get a little tired of the same portrayals. Like a headline I saw recently with the words 'lifting the veil on the Arab world' juxtaposed next to a veiled face and a pair of mysterious eyes. I can assure you, we Arab women are not that mysterious!"

"Do you know that you have a different CNN than we have?" Salah al Shuroogi asked me. "CNN in the U.S. (CNN National) is different than CNN (International) in the rest of the world, and so is CNBC. I bet your CNN doesn't have *Discover Middle East* on it. *Discover Middle East* is about how Arabs live and the Arab world in general."

"The real thing is that we easily can know what's going on in America," said Nofa al Sulaiti. "We can easily get your news; we easily can have a lot of information about you, but it's very difficult and very hard for you in America to know what's going on in the real world in the Middle East or in Bahrain. The only news that is broadcast to you over there is the war; how many people get killed daily. But there's nothing about the good news or the technology coming out of the Middle East; they won't broadcast that."

AMERICAN Generalization #10

Arabs as a whole are judged as terrorists and radicals, because this is what is in the news.

If you listen to the Bahraini Arab Muslims, they will tell you that the American and Western media as a whole have been demonizing the Arab and the Muslim world in general. While the American media is quick to point out its freedom of expression and speech, the Bahrainis contend that the same powerful media refuses to extend its freedom of expression on matters it deems sensitive.

"I think in terms of the U.S., the above generalization is probably right," Nader Shaheen commented. "When you are talking about America as a ruling nation, which it is, unfortunately I think it is far too defined by its cities. It's LA, New York, Chicago – but most people live in the country. The majority of Americans don't live in the big cities; they live outside of them.

"The Midwestern experience is very different from the Florida experience. As somebody in Minnesota, you would be more aware perhaps of generally what Arabs represent. Stylized Arabs is one view that is deeply ingrained and has been by non-Arabs. Arabs are still portrayed in the movies and TV as villains -- the guys to be shot, and the guys to be hacked up.

"The Homeland Security Act, the National Security Act, the Patriot Act; all of these are to curb the rights of Americans, not Muslims. How is that not an attack?" questioned Shaheen. "The easiest thing to do in the world would be to drive a car down Wall Street, take it off the road and onto the pavement, and you'll kill hundreds of people if you want to. But that hasn't happened. There haven't been shootings by Muslims, yet you can buy a gun anywhere in the States. That would be the easiest way for a Muslim who wanted to express his ire or discord with American foreign policy to do – off Americans – and that hasn't happened.

"I think it is important to look at not what has happened, but what hasn't happened. How widespread is a movement to attack the United States? I think your Texas Republican president just knee-jerk reacts in that way, saying that they're all (Arab Muslims) in it, and they're all doing it. It's not true, and those aren't the facts."

"I realize we have perceptions about each other that will never be dispelled in our lifetime," said Toni Grundstrom, a Minnesotan. "It's hard to form an honest opinion about the Arab people when all you hear is what the media wants you to hear. When you listen to the local news, all they report about are the 'bad guys.' It is the same everywhere. The 'bad guys' get the publicity, and those who want to live good lives, be kind and help one another are NEVER recognized. I will not lump all Middle Eastern citizens in the 'bad guy' category, regardless of how the media portrays them."

Dave Everson, another Minnesotan, wondered aloud how Americans can better understand the Bahraini Muslims, Islam, and its teachings if all we see are the negative images portrayed on television of people in the streets burning American flags and protesting against the American government. "I know that we need to work hard to distance the radicals from the everyday Bahraini Arab and learn more about their religion."

› The Bahraini Arabs
dress like Americans,
watch your movies,
listen to your music...
but they are Arabs with
their own culture, too.
It's their version of
the American dream. ‹

Lee Ann Fleetwood

CHAPTER 8

Understanding and Promoting Cross-Cultural Awareness

At a time when many Muslims consider themselves at war with America, the clash of cultures needs to be addressed. Understanding and tolerance is the order of the day on both sides. It takes dedicated effort to build cultural bridges, particularly when things, such as cartoons and teddy bears, so easily destroy these efforts. Many Americans are completely baffled as to why the big hoopla about a teacher naming a teddy bear Muhammad. Her action, intended to be respectful, instead was considered a crime against Islam, and the American airwaves did not hesitate to voice their shock and dismay.

In today's multicultural world, where there is less respect for individuals and collective human life as well as more dangerous world tension and increased pain and suffering, everyone needs to not only be aware of, but also do their part to combat these social injustices. Americans need to understand that Arabs have their own culture and traditions, which are very different from ours, yet there does not need to be a conflict between the groups.

ARAB Generalization #11

Americans know nothing about Bahrain, or even where Bahrain is. They probably think we still live in tents in the desert and ride camels.

True, admitted Nader Shaheen, responding to the Arab generalization. "And that's our [media] fault. It's really right off the playground. But to be perfectly honest with you, there wasn't much to tell. We export oil and that's about it."

"Just tell them it's the former home of Michael Jackson. They can relate to that," a Muslim man told me unable to keep a straight face in the process.

The Americans I interviewed overwhelmingly agreed with the above Arab generalization. On average, Americans know nothing about Bahrain. Many I spoke with didn't even know that the United States Navy's Fifth Fleet is headquartered in Bahrain and has been for more than fifty years.

America has always had a tradition of isolationism, Bahraini Arabs believe, but opinions were split as to Americans lacking knowledge about Bahrain specifically and the international world in general.

"That's the problem; we know more about you than you know about yourselves," stated Salah al Shuroogi. "We know where your fleet is, where your armies are stationed..."

"We talk about our nature; our culture," explained Shaikh Ahmed bin Isa bin Khalifa al Khalifa, assistant undersecretary of Nationality, Passports and Residence in Bahrain. "We've got people from all sectors of the Gulf living in Bahrain--Bahrainis who are Iranian descent, Persian descent--but Bahrain being as it is, it sort of merges all of these people and comes up with the Bahraini person. Those with Arab or Persian descent have no demarcation amongst them. The nice thing was that Bahrain School encompassed that in such a way for not only the local area, but also for people who came from the United States, Europe, Australia, or Japan. We interacted not in school, but outside of school. Slowly but surely, this has changed in view of the changes in the world we live in.

"The gap started widening," he continued. "There is a strong sense these days that we are experiencing sectarianism, even within the Gulf itself, and the people themselves. We used to live in areas where we didn't look into a person's background in terms of whether he was Sunni, Shiite, Buddhist, or Christian. Bahrain once had a large community of Jewish people, and there was a synagogue here. If you walk into the old Suq, you can find a Buddhist temple. We had no problems with people of different faiths. But somehow the division started to appear. People started whining to themselves and creating these divides, and now it's happening outside; it's unfortunate.

"Maybe it was the effect of the '70s; it was in the '80s when people were confused, because they were caught in between two generations. You saw it in the '90s," Shaikh Ahmed stated. "Now it's commonplace. It used to be something that you didn't talk about, and now it's something that is talked about in gatherings and majlises [meeting places]. It's something similar to the homogenous interaction between all sects. You have Indians, Shiites, Sunnis, and you have different sects, and they all interacted. Nobody ever talked about this area being Shiite and this area Sunni. My Sunni aunt used to live in a Shiite area; I never thought about it until now. How come I'm thinking about it now? My aunt--being who she was and living amongst them--until this day, people who remember her think of her fondly. But at the time, I was young and when we went to visit her, we didn't think of the neighbors being Shiite or whatever; we knew them as people. So we didn't start branding until it came into this era unfortunately," he admitted. "You didn't see kids talk about it, and now they talk about it in school. 'This is my friend who is Shia.' You try to instill in them that there is no difference between any sect; everybody worships God in their own way, but unfortunately society forces you into compartmentalization and people feel safer that way. They had something to relate to, I guess, that they are part of something. But Bahrain never used to be like this."

"No problem. This is not a bad thing," said Wafaa Ashoor about the American generalization. "Yeah, we live in a desert. When someone mentions Kenya to me, because I have not been there, I think they are living in a field with lions around them, because that's what I've seen in the movies and on TV. They aren't portrayed accurately."

In the past, few American politicians traveled internationally, but that has changed. Lawmakers now seem to understand that they need to have a broader idea of what's happening in the world beyond the U.S. borders.

Salah al Shuroogi, shaking his head, said he is in disbelief whenever he watches The Tonight Show with Jay Leno on satellite. "Leno goes out onto the street and asks random Americans questions about history or their culture. Their ignorant answers are pretty shocking."

AMERICAN Generalization #11

Muslims think Americans are not tolerant of their religion or their culture, particularly post 9/11.

"I think the media has a lot to do with this statement," said al Shuroogi. "Actually, they increased the hate."

"If you are honest, you'll find lots of Americans who still dislike Arabs because of what happened on 9/11," said Rasool Hassan. "But can you say this is right? Americans are very well educated and are powerful around the world. Do you think this is the way they think? Do you expect this from well-educated people? For example, my family and I live here in Bahrain. Let's say someone from our family went and killed someone. Do you think all of us are bad like him? This is what happened with 9/11.

"I am a Muslim, and I'm telling you that what bin Laden did was wrong. Islam does not believe in killing innocent people. Who is bin Laden to play God?

"We need to highlight the good," he continued. "If one guy made a mistake, that shouldn't mean everybody has to pay for it. Have there been any Bahrainis bothering you or doing anything bad toward you while you've been in Bahrain? Have you found Bahrainis good people or bad people?

"I'll tell you a story. We had a problem maybe five or ten years ago. A group of American soldiers came to Bahrain from Saudi Arabia. For six months they had had nothing to drink. When they arrived in Bahrain, they went to the Gulf Hotel and drank until they were fully drunk. Then this group went out and broke into cars, hit people and got into fights. Do you think I'm going to say all Americans are very bad because of this example? We need to be fair with each other [Americans and Arab Muslims] and realize that some will point fingers at us and others will not."

My experience during the times that I've been in Bahrain was very positive overall. I found Bahrainis to be wonderful people. They are friendly, helpful, and don't seem to pass judgment on me as an American. There have been Bahrainis who have gone out of their way to assist me and/or my husband when we needed information or help navigating Bahraini red tape and regulations. I can honestly say that I am very tolerant of the Bahraini Muslims and their culture. As a Christian, I have no right to pass judgment on an entire culture for the acts of a few. I am not God; let Him judge. Life is too short to hold grudges or bear hatred.

That said, I have realized, as well as heard from those I interviewed, that Bahrainis have a difficult time differentiating between Americans and the American government.

"I personally feel that Americans don't accept us," said Abdulla al Sada. "If there is any problem now because of the United States, the first finger pointed is toward the Arabs. Why is that? I really would like to know. People here in the Middle East feel that the Europeans are more diplomatic than the Americans because of our experience with the colonies. America is always taking things by force. Life is not like that. Some day there will be a power shift and America will be weak. It may take two hundred or four hundred years to happen, but it will happen. You should not make enemies for yourself just because you are strong now."

"We didn't say we were perfect. We make mistakes, and we have our problems," admitted Maryam al Sheroogi. "We don't want Americans to make us out to all be terrorists and bad people."

Wafaa Ashoor suggested that there is give and take on this particular generalization. "I have met many Americans who have come to teach at the school where I teach, and what is stated in this generalization is exactly what they think when they first arrive. But once we talk with each other, they understand, and then completely erase what they originally thought about Muslims."

"You have to be honest, and you have to be fair in what you say," Rasool Hassan said. "I cannot blame the whole nation just because of one guy who made the mistake. And this is now happening in America, to be very honest with you, especially after the eleventh of September.

"Truthfully, as a Muslim I'm thinking the same way as Americans thought. I can say Americans are really bad people, I hate them, don't trust them, and I don't ever want to see them. Ask me why I think that, and I will tell you it is because of what they have done in Iraq. It's simple to feel that way. What I have just said is what I think Americans in general think about us because of 9/11. I can say that I'm from Bahrain and have nothing to do with Iraq, just as the Bahrainis had nothing to do with the terrorist attacks on 9/11. Americans need to forget that we are Muslim or not Muslim; we are human. I am human, and you are human. I don't care if you pray or don't pray. Be polite, talk to people nicely, so they will respond nicely. It's simple. It's something people of all religions can do."

"There are circumstances one can point to that collaborate the reasoning behind American Generalization #11," according to Shaheen. "For example, Britain captured eleven suicide bomber terrorists – Muslims – and all of a sudden no one is allowed to take any liquid on aircrafts anymore because it is a possible way someone can cause death and destruction.

"That thinking still prevails; clear plastic, quart-size re-sealable bags with liquids and gels less than so many ounces," Shaheen pointed out. "Every single one of those eleven individuals arrested were released without charge over a year ago, but I still can't send jam to my mother, and I still can't take a bottle of water on the plane with me. There are so many mixed messages; it's no wonder nobody knows what's going on. What does that mean? We Muslims are no different than anybody else. Who benefits from that? Unfortunately for Arab folk, they view the common denominator to almost every single one of these mini events to be in some way attached or associated with you as foreign host, and in most every case it is.

"For my money, the American opinion of the Arabs is all based in lies, lack of facts, and ignorance, and none of it is true," contended Shaheen. "Yet an entire opinion is formed on the basis of that. I think some in the American media are intolerant but, by and large, I think the United States is extremely tolerant of Muslims. And most Muslims that I know are aware of that. There are the prejudices and some intolerance, but who could blame them given all the crap Americans have been fed by the media and by your politicians. I can't blame people for thinking that way. But I don't think this generalization is true. America is a very liberal and tolerant country, and in many ways, very naïve, as well. You can be exploited and over-exploited, and America has been exploited, not least of all by the people that are supposed to represent you. And that really, really rankles me, because my experience with Americans by and large is that they are very trusting and very honest people.

"So do the Muslims have a legitimate argument here or is it just more conspiracy theories? Arabs find themselves trying to defend their very existence based on the fact that nineteen terrorists attacked the United States in 2001, and others have been arrested as part of terrorist cells in different countries. The U.S. is a very huge and mighty country, and we are powerless to do anything about it.

"Again, I go back to these Islamist extremists who preach death. There is no stopping someone from taking a piece of religion and turning it into his own hands, and proclaiming 'I do this in the name of Islam.' You can't stop anyone from doing that. You couldn't stop David Karesh and the Branch Dividians from doing it in Waco, Texas; you couldn't stop Jim Jones in Guyana who took everyone down there in a mass suicide attempt with Kool-Aid laced with poison. Timothy McVeigh in Oklahoma couldn't be stopped. If some nut case has got it in his head that he's going to change the world by blowing himself up, he is going to do it, and there's nothing you and I can do about it. But what America and other western countries are saying is, okay, you Muslims need to reform your religion. It took the West two hundred years and got them an ungodly inquisition. It can't happen in the four or eight years that you are president, or in forty years."

"I think the only thing you can do is stop listening to people who make generalizations like this, and try not to be influenced by it," recommended Shaikh Ahmed. "You have to go back to the U.S. People thought we Arabs would have a hard time being in the United States after 9/11. But we don't. Public perception--that's the problem. Seriously, I thought there would be problems after 9/11, but there are no problems. No one was hassled. You have the TSA, but they are always high-strung people. You only break up this misconception that Americans aren't tolerant of us by going to America. You can't sit and be influenced by whatever is being projected, whether it be the news or the views... you have to go see for yourself.

"For a certain time after 9/11 it was difficult for Arabs to get a visa to the United States," continued Shaikh Ahmed, "But that's no longer true. There was a time last year or maybe even in 2006 that anybody named Ahmed or Mohammed couldn't get a visa, which affected a lot of people obviously. Unfortunately, the U.S. Embassy here in Bahrain cannot tell you why that was. It was something dictated by Homeland Security. Homeland Security is tough. But now that's over."

How Other World Countries View Muslims

Results of the Harris Interactive Survey, which were published in the *Financial Times* on August 21, 2007, indicated that British respondents overall viewed Muslims as a whole with more suspicion than their American or European counterparts. Survey results showed that more than fifty-two percent of Britons believed a "major terrorist attack" would occur in their country within the next twelve months, which was the highest proportion of any of the countries surveyed – Britain, France, Germany, Spain, Italy, and the U.S. – compared to thirty percent of Americans and thirty-two percent of Spanish answering the same question. Additionally, more than forty-six percent of Britons felt that Muslims had too much political power, compared to a third of Italians and Germans, and less than a quarter of Spaniards, and a fifth of Americans. A large majority of the French do not see Muslims as a threat, and were the most enthusiastic when asked if they saw Muslims as suitable marriage partners for their children. In Spain, fewer than a quarter viewed Muslims as a threat, while a fifth said they would oppose Muslims marrying their children. In the U.S., only twenty-one percent of respondents saw Muslims as a threat, although more than forty percent said they would oppose their children marrying Muslims.

Attitudes of U.S. Muslims

In the U.S., the Pew Research Center[4] conducted a first ever, comprehensive nationwide survey of nearly sixty thousand Muslim Americans in an attempt to measure their demographics, attitudes, and experiences between January and April 2007. The results, released in May 2007, indicated that,

[4]*www.people-press.org/reports/display.php3?ReportID=329*

overall, Muslim Americans are mostly mainstream and middle class. That is, the Muslim American population is youthful, racially diverse, generally well-educated, and financially about as well-off as the rest of the U.S. public. The Pew Research Center concluded they are "largely assimilated, happy with their lives, and moderate with respect to many of the issues that have divided Muslims and the Westerners around the world."

The survey also contrasted the views of the Muslim population as a whole with those of the U.S. general population, and with the attitudes of Muslims around the world, including Western Europe.

Overall, the poll found that American Muslims are more likely than their European counterparts to reject Islamic extremism and expressed satisfaction with their lives. Two-thirds (sixty-five percent) of adult Muslims living in the U.S. are foreign-born as compared to thirty-five percent U.S.-born. Of the foreign-born Muslims, twenty-four percent are from Arab countries. Of the thirty-five percent of U.S.-born Muslims, twenty-one percent are converts to Islam, compared to fourteen percent born Muslim. Not so surprising was that "the younger Muslims in the U.S. are more likely than older Muslim Americans to express a strong sense of Muslim identity, and are much more likely to say that suicide bombings in the defense of Islam can be at least sometimes justified."

The survey results also stated that, in general, the Muslim Americans surveyed were not reluctant to express discontent with the U.S. war on terrorism and the impact it has had on their lives. The majority of them (fifty-three percent) indicated it is more difficult to be a Muslim in this country since the September 11 terrorist attacks. Although most believed that the government singles out Muslims for profiling and surveillance, seventy-three percent stated they had never experienced discrimination while living in the U.S.

"Relatively few Muslim Americans believe the U.S.-led war on terror is a sincere effort to reduce terrorism," states the survey results, with views mirroring the strong disapproval Muslims in the Middle East have voiced regarding the "war on terrorism."

The majority of those surveyed believed that Muslims immigrating to the States "should try and adopt American customs rather than trying to remain distinct from the larger society." One of the most positive views, by nearly two-to-one (sixty-three percent to thirty-two percent), is that Muslim Americans do not see a conflict between being a devout Muslim and living in a modern society.

Because the U.S. Census is forbidden by law to ask about religious affiliation, there are no generally accepted projections of the size of the Muslim American population. However, the Pew Study estimates approximately one and a half million adult Muslim Americans (age eighteen and older) reside in the U.S.

Nearly half (forty-seven percent) of U.S. Muslims consider themselves Muslim first and American second. When compared with Muslims living in Britain, France, Germany and Spain, Muslim Americans felt that life is better for women in the U.S. as opposed to the other four countries.

One area Muslim Americans' views were similar to those of the general U.S. public was with the Israel/Palestinian issues. "Muslim Americans are far more likely than Muslims in the Middle East and elsewhere to say that a way can be found for the state of Israel to exist so that the rights of the Palestinians are addressed," states the study.

Overwhelmingly, and not surprisingly, six-to-one (seventy-five percent vs. twelve percent) Muslim Americans oppose the war in Iraq. Only one percent felt that suicide bombings against civilian targets were often justified to defend Islam; an additional seven percent polled said suicide bombings are sometimes justified in these circumstances. Those who said that suicide bombings in defense of Islam can be often or sometimes justified are more disbelieving than others that Arabs carried out the September 11 attacks.

Finally, data from Minnesota Muslims was compiled and studied. Despite flare-ups over Somali Muslims refusing to scan pork at supermarket checkouts and transport passengers who have alcohol with them in taxis, Minnesota Muslims reflect the general U.S. Muslim poll findings. "Co-existence is definitely an option" was the Minnesota finding regarding immigrant experience in the United States.

U.S. Representative Keith Ellison of Minnesota, the first Muslim to serve in Congress, described the message to be taken from the Pew survey as being, "The United States has lessons to teach the world about inclusion. Maybe the good old United States is doing something right. Having gone through a civil war, having gone through Jim Crow, having gone through a women's rights movement... we've learned something about the value of tolerance."

What Minnesotans and the U.S. are Doing to Promote Understanding and Tolerance

The Islamic Center of Minnesota is located in Fridley, Minnesota, a Minneapolis suburb. The Muslim Youth of Minnesota host annual events, such as the 2007 Chocolate Spring Fling. The events are organized with the purpose of creating dialogue and educating non-Muslims about the Muslim culture and faith, in an attempt to build bridges. Activities at events such as the Chocolate Spring Fling included applying henna to hands, Arabic name-writing demonstrations, viewing educational movies, prayer demonstrations, and presentations on Islam.

Located within the Fridley Islamic Center is Al-Amal School, the state's only full-time Islamic school. The school shares classes with a nearby Catholic high school where a Muslim teacher in particular has become a close friend to a science teacher at the Catholic school. Both report close ties and have even co-taught combined classes. The school also arranges for the Muslim students to use its outdoor athletic facilities.

Although Normandale Community College in Bloomington, another Minneapolis suburb, has a designated "meditation room" that Muslim students share with other religious faiths, confrontations have developed over the sex-segregated room, which the Muslim students prefer. The major issue raised by some students is that sex-segregation presents a constitutional problem in a public educational institution and, since this meditation room is open to all students, non-Muslims resent the segregated area along with the posted signs instructing them to remove their shoes. Problems are expected to arise when something unprecedented is put into action, although some college faculty feel the meditation room has essentially become a Muslim prayer room, which they think extends beyond religious toleration.

Minneapolis Community and Technical College (MCTC) is the first public institution in Minnesota to install wudu (ritual bathing) facilities for Muslim students. According to MCTC president Phil Davis, "It's a simple matter of extending hospitality to newcomers. It's no different than providing a fish option in the college cafeteria for Christian students during Lent."

The project is using the Muslim Accommodations Task Force website as a primary resource. This task force's eventual objectives on American campuses, according to their website, include: permanent Muslim prayer spaces, ritual washing facilities, separate food and housing for Muslim students, separate hours at athletic facilities for Muslim women, paid imams or religious counselors, and campus observance of Muslim holidays.

Interest in Arabic surged among Americans following the 9/11 attack, and hundreds of U.S. college students have enrolled in American-affiliated Middle East colleges since then in an attempt to learn more about the people, their culture, and religion. For many, it is an opportunity to learn Arabic, study Islam, and slice through media stereotypes as they prepare for careers in intelligence or diplomacy. One American student said she came to the Middle East to understand the widespread anger in the region over U.S. policies. Most say the Arab world does not resemble the violent place the U.S. media often portrays. A twenty-two-year-old American student named Ken said, "I wanted to be introduced to Islam and know the people on a for-real basis, not based on the headlines."

Jackson, another American student, thinks 9/11 was a wake-up call of sorts. "The United States as a whole has learned that we need to get serious about learning about other cultures and languages in general."

"People think everyone here is a terrorist or they hate you because you are Christian," a former Baylor student told a Reuters reporter. "That's not the case. When I get back, I am going to tell my friends that these are good people."

In July 2007, President George W. Bush announced at a speech to the Organization of the Islamic Conference (OIC) marking the fiftieth anniversary of the Islamic Center of Washington, a mosque and Islamic cultural center in the U.S. capitol, that the U.S. government was creating a post for a special envoy to the largest Islamic bloc. The result would "hopefully contribute to strengthening the dialogue between the United States and the OIC" in addition to representing a major step "towards a historical reconciliation between the West and the Muslim world."

The U.S. State Department released its 2007 report late that same year on International Religious Freedom, praising the Kingdom of Bahrain for its religious freedom. It stated that Bahrain is maintaining its status of providing freedom to believers to follow their religion without government interference. The report also highlighted that religious literature was openly sold in local bookstores where Islamic holy books are sold.

Building cultural bridges nationally from a business standpoint, the U.S. State Department invited five businesswomen from Bahrain to participate in the Women Business Leaders Summit in the U.S. in July 2007. The purpose of the forum was to introduce fifty businesswomen from ten Arab countries to fifty businesswomen from all fifty of the U.S. states to establish a partnership between one Arab and one U.S. businesswoman in the same business line. The five-day "shadow" program aimed to identify working procedures and modern techniques in business. In addition to the forum, the Bahraini businesswomen spent time with First Lady Laura Bush, visited the U.S. Congress where they met female members of Congress, attended various functions, and met other influential U.S. businesswomen.

The 2008 US/Bahrain Youth Citizenship for Disability Inclusion Exchange Program, administered by Mobility International USA and sponsored by the U.S. Department of State, kicked off in March 2008. The three-week international exchange program brought together a delegation of teenagers with and without physical disabilities from the U.S. and Bahrain. The program objectives are to strengthen the bonds of friendship, cultural respect, and understanding between young people in the U.S. and Bahrain, as well as to provide opportunities for participants to explore and develop leadership skills in their communities and countries.

From an educational perspective, a number of U.S. college professors and U.S. Muslim leaders visited Bahrain in the past year, conducting lectures promoting cultural understanding between Islam and the West. Some of these visits have been organized by Bahraini organizations, whereas others have come on their own or by invitation of the U.S. Embassy in Bahrain.

The Cordoba Initiative, an independent, non-partisan, and multinational project co-founded in 2002 by New York-based imam Feisal Abdul Rauf, works with states and non-states to improve Muslim-West relations. Describing The Cordoba Initiative as a think-tank, Imam Feisal said they craft strategies and find ways to implement them, strategically working together, partnering with stakeholders, and leveraging their capacity to achieve specific results toward bridging the divide between the Arab world and the West. When Imam Feisal spoke in Bahrain in October 2007, however, he cautioned the audience that it might take another one or two U.S. administrations before relations between the West and Muslims start to improve noticeably.

In one of his speeches, the Muslim scholar acknowledged that, in the aftermath of 9/11, Americans took notice of Islam and wanted to know more about Muslims and their religion. "The goodwill generated was tremendous," Feisal said. He explained that since the September 11, 2001, attacks, American questions about the Arab world and Islam fell into three categories: What is Islam? Why is Osama bin Laden popular in the Muslim world? [The Bahrainis I spoke with said bin Laden is hated in the majority of the Muslim world] and, What can Americans do together as non-Muslims and Muslims to bring about a real change?

Feisal called upon better media communication noting that the perceptions of Islam and the rest of the world is largely informed by the media, and a need for American senators and congressmen to be better informed about the Muslim world.

The last few years have witnessed members of Congress and the Senate making more trips to Middle Eastern Arab countries in an effort to learn more about the Muslim world and culture.

Mary Darling, a Minnesota native and executive producer of a Canadian sitcom entitled "Little Mosque on the Prairie", a take off on "The Little House on the Prairie" about Laura Ingalls Wilder's life growing up on the Minnesota plains, puts Muslims in a sitcom that is wildly popular in Canada. Darling has been trying to bring the sitcom to the U.S. The sitcom, she believes, "normalizes" Muslims living among non-Muslims as a way of dispelling stereotypes by humanizing the Muslim character in a positive way. A number of Bahraini Muslims who have seen clips of the show on You Tube, however, disagree with the character portrayals as being "normalized."

"Since 9/11, Muslims have been portrayed in America in terms of conflict that creates a one-dimensional perception of the Muslim community," said the sitcom's creator Zarqa Nawaz. "I simply want people to laugh with Muslims like they would laugh at anyone else--and feel comfortable doing so."

How Bahrain is Promoting Cross-Cultural Relations

"Bahrain is a multicultural society, and has been open to many cultures for centuries," Sunni businessman Abdulla al Sada said. "We don't harbor any segregation toward people whether they are Americans, British, Indians or anyone else who is in our country. We are all working and living peacefully with each other. Some societies accept others more readily, and then there are those societies that feel you are lower than they, so they don't accept you. I don't believe there is that much of a cultural gap between our two countries. There is a much wider gap between America and nations such as Iran, Iraq, and Palestine."

"We know that the American policy is one thing, and the American people are another – two totally separate entities that don't come in together," Shaikh Ahmed explained. "You only learn that through communication, education, and sending people abroad. The Crown Prince's International Scholarship Program banks on people and, no matter what sect they come from, these are Bahrainis and this is the direction of His Majesty. They go out to the outside. His objective is even if they work abroad; they are projecting what Bahrainis are for people coming into Bahrain. He will eventually come back; people don't usually stay out of the country forever. There is something about Bahrain that brings Bahrainis back.

"So he is educating his friends and, at the end of the day, we're getting the benefit of that. If he is influenced by the outside and brings it back into Bahrain, so be it – all the best for Bahrain," concluded Shaikh Ahmed.

Many Bahraini and American leaders and organizations are increasingly embracing the challenge of understanding the need for fostering cross-cultural awareness between our two countries.

In March 2007, then Information Minister Dr. Mohammed Abdul Ghaffar called for the public relations industry in the Gulf States (Bahrain, Saudi Arabia, Kuwait, Oman, Qatar, United Arab Emirates) to accept the unique opportunity to help correct misconceptions about Muslims and their faith in the Western world.

"The phenomenon of Islamophobia, especially after the events of September 11, is a clear example of how a whole country can be tarnished and stained by the actions of a few of its citizens," Ghaffar said.

"Some nations are under the assumption that all Muslims support all the actions taken in the name of Islam. Although most Muslims view terrorists to be in breach of Islamic laws, they suffer from being associated with these terrorists and murderers.

"Pubic relations could help portray how Islam is a dynamic and diverse faith with internal debates and developments. Understanding each other will help us to see eye to eye and hopefully live in a more peaceful world.

"It's very important that Bahrain's textbooks and teachers promote respect and love of other races through their teachings, beginning with the very youngest preschool children. Children must be taught in the home, mosque, and schools that it is evil to hate other human beings. Granted, it is going to take twenty or more years for this to firmly become ingrained, but it must begin now. The next few upcoming generations will then have grown up in that very public (and hopefully home-taught private) atmosphere and attitude that hatred of another is wrong. Islam does not promote it, nor does Christianity. Mankind will always have philosophical, religious, and political disagreements, but hatred should never be part of that mix."

"Create a world without hate" was the message of Bahrain's Foreign Minister Shaikh Khalid bin Ahmed Al Khalifa to the United Nations General Assembly in the fall of 2007. He urged nations to steer away from hatred, and racial and discriminatory conflicts. "Such conflicts are caused by fear of Islam, or what has become known as Islamophobia, which some try to promote to cause sedition and hatred among peoples to achieve petty political designs," he said.

U.S.-based Arab American Institute founder and president Dr. James Zogby addressed a public relations conference in Bahrain in March 2007. He suggested that growing trade and investment, and political cooperation, had done little to promote an understanding of the culture and history of Muslims. He noted that a negative attitude toward Arabs is still prevalent. "The so-called experts and anti-Arab journalists helped to recycle negative stereotypes and present them as new information in the aftermath of September 11. We Arab-Americans were caught in the middle of our own dilemma." Dr. Zogby added that there is also much to be hopeful for, as the American people have shown a keen interest in learning more about the Arab world and its people.

In March 2007, Discover Islam, in cooperation with the Hamad Town Charity Fund, organized a festival with a focus on Islamic culture as part of the events for the prestigious Formula One race held in the Kingdom. With such an influx of visitors from other countries, organizers felt the festival, which aimed to address negative stereotypes visitors may have toward Islam and the Bahraini Muslims, was the ideal venue. Now in its fourth year, the festival has proven to be a popular attraction.

"Most visitors are grateful to learn about the religion," a Discover Islam spokesman said. "Most have many questions and are misinformed because they get much of their information from television, which tends to focus on terrorism and women's issues. We do our best to teach them about the reality of Islam and the tolerance of the religion."

Another example of building harmony through dialogue takes place annually at the Grand Mosque on Bahrain's National Day (December 16) and during Eid Al Fitr, which marks the end of Ramadan. Organizers host an Open House festival featuring various activities, such as learning Arabic phrases, sampling Arabic sweets, henna paintings, and offering non-Muslim foreigners the opportunity to experience Arabian hospitality. Their objective is to promote better understanding and harmony between different faiths and cultures through friendly coexistence.

Religious tour guide Nejma Mohammed Naeem said that most visitors to the mosque are from the West, with thirty percent being the U.S. American servicemen stationed with the Navy's Fifth Fleet in Bahrain that visit the Grand Mosque as part of their orientation program when they arrive on the island.

"A Fruitful Exchange" proclaims the *Bahrain City Tribune* headline of June 27, 2007. Four U.S. college students were invited to the Kingdom by various businesses where they worked and interacted both on personal and business levels with Bahrainis.

James and Eric found the experience an "eye opener." Eric felt that "in this part of the world, relationships matter a lot. It is very different compared to how things are done back home. It is obvious that family matters a lot here. The image we get back home is so distorted. It is obvious the media has an agenda."

James observed that "interaction between different cultures is vital to promote understanding and peace."

The four students, identified only by their first names, agreed that the experience confirmed to them that people are the same all over the world. They also felt the more such business exchanges that take place, the better. The students were laying the groundwork for a program that could lead to regular visits by students from the U.S. to Bahrain. The twofold goal of such an exchange is for human interaction barriers to be brought down, and to provide students with hands-on international experience.

Bahraini banker Nader Shaheen, who incorporates standup comedy into his corporate speeches, has developed a routine that pokes fun at himself, as a way of shaking down the image the West has of the Muslim world and Muslims in general.

For Shaheen, comedy is the tool he uses to help alter cultural perceptions held by his primarily Western audiences. "The very fact that Arabs are such a mystery in the West provides enough fodder for comedy routines," he told me.

Dr. Faisal al Hamer, Bahrain's health minister, believes that today's young people can help bring cultures together. "Those aged fifteen to twenty-four represent one-sixth of the world population, and their participation in furthering understanding between civilizations must be strengthened," he told the media in January 2008. "They [today's youth] are open-minded and result-minded. We must work together to involve them. They may succeed where we failed. Staging youth-oriented events will have an immeasurable impact in bringing other peoples and civilizations closer and will help to prevent conflicts."

"It is easy to speak about building bridges of trust, about promoting tolerance, about advancing cross-cultural friendships," emphasized UN Information Centre director Nejib Friji speaking at the first Bahrain Dialogue Among Civilizations forum in Bahrain in January 2008. "It is far harder to translate these lofty words into actions – specific actions that change what people see, what they say and, ultimately, how they act. The UN welcomes any steady progress where it counts – on the airwaves, in the classrooms, in mosques and among the young people who will lead tomorrow's world."

Despite admitting that the media has an agenda and portrays cultures in the manner they want, almost all the American and Bahraini people I spoke with agreed that real change needs to happen within the media. "We came to know about American culture through the media, just as Americans hear about us through your media," said Hameed Alawi, although quickly pointing out that therein lies the problem that spurs the growth of misconceptions and falsehoods.

How Average Bahrainis and Americans Can Do Their Part

There is much that Americans and Arab Muslims can learn from each other, as well as much to gain. During my conversations with Americans, the majority were very positive in wanting to learn more about the Bahraini Arab culture.

So what do we do as average Americans? How can an individual promote awareness? How do we change the different perceptions held by both countries?

"We need to see the similarities in both countries' people," Kathy Hanlin told me. "To see compassion, love of family, the good that people do for their community and world. I would love to have an email pen pal that shares my life situations with whom I could discuss values and perceptions. We as Americans need to be knowledgeable about different countries, and not lump all the Middle Eastern countries together. In other words, we need a history lesson."

Another American, who wished not to be named, said she truly believed that the ordinary Bahraini Muslim is kind, gentle and loving, the same as we Christians. "However, when I hear of the Arabs at Mayo Clinic in Rochester and how some of them treat the women who work there with such disrespect, it is hard not to lump them all into the same category. I try to get to know people as people and not base my views on what the media says. I want to base my views on the individuals I have met, talked with, and worked with."

"We need to educate ourselves, and try not to be too extreme in our views," Michelle LaGue observed.

"The average American can try to get over this notion that America is all that counts and the rest of the world doesn't," asserted Lee Ann Fleetwood. "Yes, America has to look out for America in some respects, but as this planet gets smaller every day, we cannot be ignorant of the rest of the world just because we think America is so great. Yes, be proud of your country, but at the same time, we have to open our minds and borders to people.

There are other cultures in this world; America is not the only culture. America doesn't even have a culture really," she added after a moment's reflection. "We're too young, and historically a melting pot."

"In all countries, there are people who do and say things some of us disagree with, but why must we continue to point fingers at entire cultures and races?" voiced another American woman. "Why can't we all just accept each other as human beings? I was raised to like or dislike someone because of who they were as a human being, not by the type of clothing they wore, their homes, bank accounts, religion, or customs."

Hameed Alawi suggested that the media must help promote cross-cultural understanding by being more objective in their reporting. "It's a slow process for sure, but I think the media could be more effective. Maybe a true documentary movie of an Arab's life so that Americans can see what we are really like."

He points out that with the Free Trade Agreement in place between the United States and Bahrain, allowing people to travel freely in companies to both countries, could help. "I think there are hopes that when Americans come to Bahrain they won't need a visa, and Bahrainis would not need a visa to visit America. That is the hope of our king's son, the crown prince."

"Without meeting the person face to face, I think it is hard to promote understanding," observed Wafaa Ashoor. "Depending on what I see in movies and on TV, this is completely different from when I met my American friend. Without meeting Americans, I don't think you can have the whole picture.

"To tell you the truth," she continued, "What I saw on the media was mostly killing and kidnapping. When I went to Disneyworld in 1995 and '99, I was holding onto my four boys every minute while counting one – two – three – four. I felt I would come back to Bahrain with three or less children. Really!

"I loved my trips to the States. The people were very nice. I remember when we stood in a queue for almost two hours to get on rides. By the time we reached the front of the line, I knew everybody in line. They were talking to me all the time or offering us food while we waited. The Americans were very friendly.

"My husband rented a car and when we wanted to drive somewhere outside of Disney, people gladly told us how to get there. I really was very surprised how friendly everyone was. But then, they are the ambassadors; they tell us about the people and their country through their actions," she concluded.

"Learning about and understanding another people's situations and circumstances will help us tolerate, better understand, and maybe even empathize with them," another Bahraini told me. "It also creates a ground for productive dialogue."

Another Bahraini woman said she felt that Middle East leaders and imams must continue to speak out against extremism.

"Education, which is long-term, begins with the very young at home and in the schools," Janet Sampson offered as a way of promoting awareness.

According to Shaikh Ahmed bin Isa bin Khalifa al Khalifa, "You have to communicate. You cannot choose sides, but rather create a level playing field for everybody to communicate and express their thoughts, because if you build up your perceptions about somebody in regards to what other people are trying to influence you, by nature, I would doubt what they say at first. But then I'll begin to believe my doubts if someone keeps telling me – and I trust this person and my relationship with him – that these people are not good. I would start to believe him because I would be seeing through his eyes. Unfortunately, that's what happens. So you have to break that. How do you do that? You look at the person, and you see that the perception you built up, based upon what other people are telling you, is wrong. And we know that."

Rasool Hassan doesn't think there are any big cultural gaps between Americans and Bahraini Arab Muslims. "To be honest, lots of Bahrainis have been to America, Canada, and the UK. They come back here and talk.

Also, the Internet cuts the gap.

"There is only one thing we need to do, and that is correct the false information that is being conveyed." He cites the example of a Bahraini visiting America and going to "bad" places, then returning to Bahrain and talking about it, which portrays the country negatively. "Maybe what we need is not to fill the gap, but clean the information conveyed."

New York Institute student Nofa al Sulaiti has an American student in some of her university classes in Bahrain as well as an American teacher. "I tell them to go ahead and ask me questions; I don't mind telling people about my culture. And I ask them things about America and they tell me. I've also chatted on the Internet with Americans, but it's kind of difficult because you don't really know who you are talking with, or if they are really American. The Americans I know are very friendly people actually. They like to help you, and I find them very easy to be with. But if I was going to school in America and wearing hijab, I'm not so sure it would be the same. I think some Americans still look at Arabs from the perspective that maybe he or she is a terrorist, and that's a little bit difficult for us."

Shaikha Haya bint Rashid Al Khalifa, former UN General Assembly president noted, "Reinforcing dialogue among civilizations and faiths is one of the most efficient tools that could be utilized to extend the bridges of understanding and passion among peoples."

A former American travel agency employee promotes world travel as a way to learn about and better understand other cultures. To illustrate her view, she read a quote from Mark Twain. "Travel is fatal to prejudice, bigotry, and narrow-mindedness, and many of our people need it solely on these accounts. Good, wholesome, charitable views of men and things cannot be acquired by vegetating in one corner of the earth all one's lifetime."

Salah al Shuroogi agreed that cultural visits are a way for the average person to do their part. He cited the yearly Formula One three-day auto racing event. "During the Formula One, loads of Americans come here to watch the race," he observed, "And the first thing they do is go to Al Fateh Mosque. We have a group of very good, well-educated, English speaking

Muslims there who are set up to talk to visitors and show them around. They don't try to convert anyone. The Americans who visit there want to know what Islam is. Discover Islam, another Muslim organization, has a tent at Formula One. We respect other religions as well. Did you know that we've had the American Anglican Church here in Bahrain for two hundred years?

"Unfortunately," he continues, "Everybody is suspect now. Even Muslims are suspect. I think some laws need to be changed in the U.S. Most students now go to the American University in the Gulf because they can't get visas to get into the U.S. to go to school. Your domestic airlines are not controlled; it is very dangerous. You can travel within the U.S. without any documents on you. This is not good. I think the FBI or police, not private companies, should handle security checkpoints. Anybody can be bribed; I think security would be more effective with government employees. With private security companies, one day an employee is here and the next day he's working in a cleaning company. And who knows what 'secrets' he tells?

"On the other hand, we have seven private universities here. Why go to the States? If you want an American education, you can get it here, and it's cheaper. Something else we must do is educate people to be more open. And the media, of course, must change, but that is difficult."

Al Shuroogi's daughter Fatima agreed. "The media is out of control. They were given the green light to do anything. It's like the bad forces are overcoming the good forces."

However it can be done, the greatest outcome of mixing diverse cultures is that we learn from each other. One of the best ways to persuade others is to listen to what they have to say, followed by direct, down-to-earth, honest dialogue.

During Ramadan 2007, my husband and I were invited to the home of an Iraqi family (Rifat Waheeb) for the iftar (breaking the fast) meal. We spent hours in deep conversation with this wonderful couple and their three teenage children, asking and answering questions about their personal experiences living in Baghdad during the war, and Muslims and Americans in general. We also talked about aspirations, fears, issues we shared in common about the world at large, and as parents raising young adults in today's volatile world – we talked about commonalities that readily brought us together. The next day, my husband received the following email from Dr. Rifat:

"We had a very nice evening yesterday with you. The kids changed their minds completely about the American people towards the perfect (positive), since they have only ideas gotten from the movies. They have found you friendly, polite, peaceful, and on the same communication level. We thank you."

GLOSSARY OF TERMS

Abaya	A black robe that women wear over their clothing
Al	Family name
Al Qaeda	The base
Archipelago	A large group of islands
Bin	Son of
Bint	Daughter of
Caliph	Muslim spiritual leader
Electoral college	A body of electors chosen to elect the president and vice president of the U.S.
Expat	An individual living and working in a foreign country
Hadith	A book of the Prophet's personal beliefs and habits
Hajj	Holy pilgrimage Muslims make to Mecca, Saudi Arabia
Halal	Something that is permitted
Haram	Something that is forbidden
Hijab	Head scarf
Imam	Holy man similar to American priest or minister
Islam	A state of being
Islamic law	Law of Islam
Mecca	Holy city in Saudi Arabia where Muslims go on Hajj
Mosque	House of prayer
Malcha/melcha	Signing of the marriage contract
Mullah	Muslim religious leader
Muslim	"Someone who is in a state of Islam" (submission to the will and law of God)
Niqab	A face covering allowing only the eyes to be seen
Quran	The holy book of Islam
Ramadan	The holy month of Islam
Salifism	Puritan viewed Islam
Sharia	Islamic law
Shia	A sect of Muslim
Sunni	A sect of Muslim
Taliban	Religious students
Wahhabis	Religious sect originating in Saudi Arabia

INDEX

A

G

H

K

L

M

N

R

S

T

W

Y

Z